DEAN —

I WANT TO THANK YOU FOR YOUR GUIDANCE, YOUR SUPPORT, AND MOST OF ALL — YOUR LEADERSHIP! I HOPE YOU ENJOY THIS READ AND CAN TAKE SOMETHING AWAY THAT YOU FEEL HAS MADE YOU BETTER. I LOOK FORWARD TO GREAT THINGS TO COME! THANK YOU!

DEVELOPING DAD

LEADING A LIFE OF LEGACY

TRENT PRESLEY

innovo
PUBLISHING
innovopublishing.com

Published by Innovo Publishing, LLC
www.innovopublishing.com
1-888-546-2111

innovo
PUBLISHING
innovopublishing.com

Publishing quality books, eBooks, audiobooks, music, screenplays & courses for the Christian & wholesome markets since 2008.

DEVELOPING DAD
Leading a Life of Legacy

Copyright © 2024 by Trent J. Presley
All rights reserved.

No part of this publication may be reproduced, stored in a retrieval system, or transmitted in any form or by any means electronic, mechanical, photocopying, recording, or otherwise, without the prior written permission of the Trent J. Presley.

Unless otherwise noted, all scripture is taken from the Holy Bible, New International Version®, NIV® Copyright ©1973, 1978, 1984, 2011 by Biblica, Inc.® Used by permission. All rights reserved worldwide.

Library of Congress Control Number: 2024918237
ISBN: 979-8-88928-039-2

Cover Design & Interior Layout: Innovo Publishing, LLC

Printed in the United States of America
U.S. Printing History
First Edition: 2024

Has God called you to create a Christ-centered or wholesome book, eBook, audiobook, music album, screenplay, or online course? Visit Innovo's educational center (cpportal.com) to learn how to accomplish your calling with excellence.

It has been said that people remember 10 percent of what we read, 20 percent of what we hear, 50 percent of what we see and hear, but 100 percent of what we feel.

This book is dedicated to my family: Trudi, Lauren, Emma, and Cam. It is my hope that they will indeed feel my love for them throughout this book. Additionally, I hope that you, as the reader, will also feel encouraged, entertained, educated, and inspired as you travel this journey.

CONTENTS

Acknowledgments ix
Foreword xi
Introduction 15

    Chapter 1: **IN THE BEGINNING**......................19
    Chapter 2: **THE STAGE IS SET**........................23
    Chapter 3: **IT'S A GIRL!** 27
    Chapter 4: **IT'S A BOY!**......................................35
    Chapter 5: **IT'S A(*NOTHER*) GIRL!**.......................43
    Chapter 6: **BEFORE . . .** 51
    Chapter 7: **TAKE MY TIME** 63
    Chapter 8: **PETS, FRIENDS, AND SPORTS**...........71
    Chapter 9: **DADS**...87
    Chapter 10: **FAITH & TRUST** 101
    Chapter 11: **WINNING AND LOSING**................107
    Chapter 12: **TURN THE PAGE . . .** 111
    Chapter 13: **EMPTY *NEXT*ING**.........................117
    Chapter 14: **SIDEWAYS**....................................123
    Chapter 15: **LOOKING AHEAD** 129
    Chapter 16: **ADVICE**...133
    Chapter 17: **ON SECOND THOUGHT . .** 139
    Chapter 18: **LEGACY** 145

About the Author 155
Book Recommendations 157

ACKNOWLEDGMENTS

It goes without saying that this book would not exist if not for my wife, Trudi, and our three kids, Lauren, Cam, and Emma. These four people make up my world. My love, admiration, and adoration for them finds depths that I hardly even know exist, but somehow I feel every bit of that depth in my heart and soul.

Trudi, my rock and my love, thank you for putting up with me not just while whittling away on this book, but through the thick and thin of our lives together. I thank God for you every single day, and without you I would simply be lost.

Lauren, my firstborn, the one who made me a dad. I love you dearly!

Cam, my one and only son. I love you dearly!

Emma, the one who completes our family. I love you dearly!

To those referenced in this book, named or unnamed, I thank you for the part you have played in my life and my story. That story is still being written, but the parts you have played to date wouldn't be complete without you. I am forever grateful and indebted to those who have tolerated me, poured into me, helped me, and, of course, loved me.

FOREWORD

When my dad first told me he was writing a book, I thought, *Wow, that's cool!* When he followed that by requesting I write the foreword, I thought, *Wow, that's intimidating!* Being that my only professional writing accomplishments at this time include a couple of B+ college essays and passing a certification test, I did not find that I was best suited for this job. Maybe one of his (many) bosses or coworkers who had made it in corporate America could give a more credentialed testament of his leadership and insight. Then, my perspective shifted. Instead of being intimidated, I started to dig into the privilege that this truly was. Who better to endorse a book about fatherhood than a product of the author's efforts?

If you know my dad, and as you read this you'll come to find out, you know that he loves sports and cars. I have lots of memories involving both individually, but there's one story in particular that combines the two that I couldn't forget even if I wanted to.

All three of us kids played a wide variety of sports as we were growing up, and my dad never missed a game. He also never failed to bring the beloved "fourth kid" with him: whatever car he was driving at the time. Likely coming from his time in the car business with his father, my dad has always been very particular about keeping his cars in tip-top shape. Interior, exterior, under the hood, the tires—you name it, it was getting the best treatment if it belonged to my dad, hence the "fourth child" designation.

One summer afternoon when I was about six or seven, and entering my time as a baseball addict, I asked my dad to play catch with me in the backyard when he got home from work. Like the great dad he is, he obliged and suggested the front yard because it was in better condition than the shaded backyard, making it more conducive for fielding ground balls. Meanwhile, sitting directly perpendicular to our throwing path was my dad's pristine, black 2000 Toyota 4Runner parked in its usual spot in the driveway. I, being the great "brother" that I am, was concerned and doubtful that this was a good idea. My dad reassured me that he trusted my accuracy

FOREWORD

and his catching ability enough that this wouldn't be an issue. Well, as a reliable seven-year-old baseball player, my third throw of the night had a little more sizzle and a lot more air than it probably should have, completely clearing my dad's head and finding the most expensive backstop I'd ever seen—the 4Runner.

We walked up to the passenger side rear door, and sure enough, a perfect baseball-sized dent had found a home on his SUV. With smoke puffing out of his ears, my dad marched inside and called it a night for our short-lived baseball outing. Looking back now, I can understand his frustration, but as a seven-year-old, I was puzzled at his anger and embarrassed at my blunder. I followed inside shortly after, visibly upset with my head hanging, and had to explain to my mom what happened.

If this were an ordinary story, it would end there, and likely, too, would my front yard catch-playing days. This story, however, possesses a lesson my dad hardwired in me from that day on: *responsibility and ownership are not to be passed off.*

Later that night, my dad approached me—his turn to be visibly upset—and apologized not only for not listening to my advice but for his anger after the situation. More than just owning up to *his* mistake, he bore the blame for *mine* as well, even encouraging me in the process. This is not only an example of an exemplary father; this is a direct reflection of God's love for us. A goal that is always at the forefront of my dad's parenting style.

In this book, I found many stories I remember well, old stories I have forgotten, and new stories I've never heard. There were plenty of audible belly laughs and actual tears shed throughout my read. While I have the unique perspective of nostalgia and the enormous benefit of growing up with these lessons instilled in me, I cannot understate the importance of the lessons learned in the following pages. Whether you are (or want to be) a mom or dad, a CEO or entry-level employee, a son or a daughter, or an athlete or a coach, or if you are just looking to learn something, this book is for you.

As you'll see, my dad can't seem to say enough about how proud he is of Lauren, Emma, and myself. Don't get me wrong here, this means the world to me. Many parents gush with pride when claiming their kids as their own. But on the flip side, it seems not as many kids

FOREWORD

reciprocate that pride when talking of their parents. That is not me. In a world where absentee fathers, whether literally or practically, run rampant and many men do not take pride in their duty as a father, my dad was always there for us. His display of passion and discipline throughout my childhood set the standard for what it means to me to "be a man." To put it plainly, my dad is my hero. He is not a *superhero*, and he is not perfect, but despite this, I consider myself beyond blessed to have a role model like him in my life each day.

There is plenty more to be said of my dad as a father, believer, businessman, salesman, leader, friend, coach, and role model, much of which can be found in the pages of this book. Observe each chapter of personal stories through your own lens of life, and unlock the countless lessons to be learned toward leading your life of legacy.

—Cam Presley

INTRODUCTION

Thank you for picking up this book. It is a labor of love that I have dreamed about for years until I finally became intentional in my efforts, inspired by God and the desire He gives me to build a lasting legacy for my family.

Over the years, I have heard the same request as many of you: *Tell me about yourself.* Many times this is in the context of a job interview (if you know me, then you know that has happened *a lot* in my life!), a social event, a school function, or as we sit along the sidelines cheering on those little ones we love so much. No matter the setting, I typically open with a quick summary of my faith and my family, all within the context of how these things make me a better person, a better employee, a better leader, and ultimately, a better dad. This book is my first but is not intended to be my last. I have working titles already on paper just waiting to be built out into works that will hopefully motivate, inspire, educate, and entertain—much the same as my prayer for this book.

In Philippians 3:12-14, Paul states,

> *Not that I have already obtained all this, or have already arrived at my goal, but I press on to take hold of that for which Christ Jesus took hold of me. Brothers and sisters, I do not consider myself yet to have taken hold of it, but one thing I do: forgetting what is behind and straining toward what is ahead, I press on toward the goal to win the prize for which God has called me heavenward in Christ Jesus.*

That is how I feel about writing this book. I most certainly have not arrived, but for my entire adult life, I have studied and sought to apply biblical principles in all I do within the confines of my family life. Always seeking to become the best dad I can be. In this book, I share, with permission, some of our family stories, my personal thoughts and feelings, and the ever-deepening love I have for my wife and kids. I know, it sounds odd for a man to actually be open to sharing his feelings and emotions, but I happily present this to you!

INTRODUCTION

As the book progresses, I will draw on the experience of these stories to share with you what I believe to be biblical truths and principles that you (no matter who you may be as you read this book) can learn and live out on your journey toward becoming the dad, the mom, the husband, the wife, that God has designed you to be. Just like me, none of us are perfect, but with God's help, grace, and strength, we can become more like the One we seek to emulate in the life we lead.

My people that you will get to know in this book are the reason behind it. Trudi, Lauren, Cam, and Emma have lived this with me over the years, and without them it would not exist. This book is dedicated to them and the love that we find through embracing each other in the good times and the bad. They are indeed my inspiration and my world, and it is my prayer that as you read this book you will be able to take away maybe a couple of things to help you lead a better life with those you love as well.

As we embark on this reading adventure together, allow me to outline a bit of the flow of this book. The purpose of this book is to help you grow and learn. To inspire you and motivate you. To make you think, to make you laugh, even to make you cry. A book about parenting and leadership and the nuance that ties these together. To provoke thoughts and plans that maybe you haven't considered before and blaze a path forward, growing closer to those you love most in your lives and deepening your relationship with the Lord. No matter your title—Dad, Mom, husband, wife, or any other title you aspire to attain one day—this book is for you!

This is a book for dads, a book for those who hope to one day be dads, a book for those looking back on life, searching for ways to make amends for time lost or mistakes made.

This is also a book for moms. Moms who are carrying a heavy load, those who are blessed beyond imagination with a godly husband, moms who are looking to help their husbands be better versions of themselves.

This book is for young adults—your whole life lies before you. Use this as a guide to help you navigate some of the pitfalls I was unable to avoid, to encourage yourself and those around you to be a better version of your/themself, to be a better husband or wife, a better leader, a better you!

INTRODUCTION

For husbands and wives who may choose to read this together: use this as a working document serving as a relationship builder! I'm confident you will find relatable stories within these pages that will spin up conversations that seem familiar yet provoking. Build on that!

As you begin to read, you will find stories from my life meant to entertain and draw you in. The book starts in this methodology and transitions into chapters that will offer experience, advice, and continued motivation, all purposed to propel you forward in your walk with each other, navigating the good and the bad that this life presents. As you travel this path, it is my desire that you enjoy the ride, culminating with a collection that will hopefully entertain, educate, and cause you to contemplate and ultimately draw closer to those you love and to the Lord.

I have a personal mission statement that is quite simple: *To help others lead their best life possible, if they only knew it existed.* That is a two-part quest: share practical and applicable tactics to live a great life, but dive in and help those who are struggling to find their way as well. Believe me, if I am an expert in anything, it could be searching for that existence of fulfillment within that life! Trial and error, falling down yet refusing to quit and getting right back up, walking the path least traveled—all of these things play a part in helping those within my circle of influence. And now . . . guess what? *You* are a person within my circle of influence by choosing to read this book. Let's enjoy this adventure together, and for any and all of the embarrassing stories I may share about my journey so far with my family, well, just know it is all in good fun. As we press forward, never forget: *the best is yet to come!*

Chapter 1

IN THE BEGINNING

It is Christmas morning, 1992. My new bride and I have just returned from our honeymoon, marking day six of this blissful union of marriage. And I have a plan. How fun would it be to take my wife on a scavenger hunt, building with each stop toward the culmination of the big present I have for her in celebrating our first Christmas together? It goes something like this . . . .

I hand her a small, simple box, and as she tentatively tears into it, she finds the first in a series of notes that will lead her around our tiny apartment, looking in cabinets, closets, and drawers, even taking a trip outside into the cold winter morning with snow spitting enough that we claim it as a white Christmas. All of this while building the anticipation toward the big reveal! It was a six-step process, and then the moment had arrived. Her final note instructed her to her last stop, and as that door opened, there it was: her brand new, beautiful, shiny, cherry red . . . *Dirt Devil vacuum cleaner.*

Yes, I did that. So in fact, it is no minor miracle that I even have the opportunity to write this book today, where I chronicle our life and adventures of raising kids and living life together! Of course, she feigned delight in her typical fashion of gratitude and appreciation rather than leaving me on the spot; what an incredible woman God put in my life to be my wife! And what an idiot I really must be to think that she would enjoy a scavenger hunt building up to a common household appliance the day after returning from our honeymoon. I'll unpack the beauty, grace, patience, and love that Trudi has shown me over the years further as we walk down this path together.

Digging in, I simply don't have the words. I realize that is an odd line for the opening chapter in a book of which I am the author, but if you are already a parent, then you know what I mean! Dating, marriage, jobs, kids, family, and all that goes with all of it! At the time of the first printing of this book, my bride and I will have celebrated nearly thirty-two years of marital bliss. I say *bliss*, but she might have another take on that! I say often that I have my hands full with that guy I see looking back at me in the mirror each day, so my wife takes on a double, no, make that a triple, dose of that and all that it entails. Full disclosure, she is the most godly, humble, discerning, and patient woman I know—truly the love of my life and the author of all things good that our kids exhibit!

Let's talk about how we met. It was 1989, and I was a junior in college when she came in as a freshman. At that time I was dating someone else, but God's plan was already in the works from the moment I laid eyes on my future bride! I remember the very first conversation I had with her. We were at a basketball game, and through a funny situation involving one of my roommates who was completely oblivious to our antics, we ended up laughing and talking through the entire game. She was sitting behind me and to my left, so I completely ignored the game as I became more and more infatuated with this beautiful girl. I went to my dorm later that night and told my roommate this very statement: "I met the girl tonight that I am going to marry!" He laughed at me and tossed me a "good luck with that" before moving on to whatever else had already caught his attention. But I did not forget that moment or that experience. I had to try.

Through a series of carefully orchestrated events, we ended up on a "date" together at one of my fraternity parties. To say this was strategic and intentional on my part would be an understatement because I was pretty sure at this point that she really didn't know what to make of me! I was older, obnoxious, and I think she was a little bit scared of me, just because of those factors. You see, to know my wife is simply to love her, and that is evident to all who are fortunate enough to be in her life. Her calm demeanor, her loving spirit, her heart for the Lord, and her ability to be the rock in a storm are just a few of the many characteristics she embodies that remind me just how blessed I am. Of course, I didn't know all of this way back then, I was just enamored by her beauty and her innocence all wrapped up in one. Believe me, I can still remember just how beautiful I thought she was the minute I laid eyes on her, and that was well before I knew any of her endearing spiritual and internal qualities.

Time passed and somehow she began to warm up to me through her college years. She actually ended up asking me to go with her to her sorority party at a pivotal point, and at that, we were off and running! We dated throughout college, and on Leap-Year Day, February 29, 1992, on the roof of the Peabody Hotel in Memphis, TN, I asked for her hand in marriage. By now you may have guessed that she said yes, making me the happiest man alive, and just under ten months later on December 19, 1992, she walked down the aisle and said "I do." With my dad as my best man, and her dad walking her down the aisle to give her away, we had more years of love and advice between them than we could have ever realized at that moment—certainly more to come on those wonderful men as we progress down this path together.

I remember our minister having to pause our ceremony for a moment, and this was completely my fault. At that moment, when I first saw Trudi coming down the aisle to join me, I was so completely overwhelmed with love, gratitude, and excitement that it simply boiled over in me. As we turned to face the minister, he saw the tears streaming down my face, and he knew I just needed a minute. There was absolutely no fear or angst on my part, just overwhelming joy, and I couldn't contain myself. Of course, as I would learn to be her norm in the years to come, Trudi was calm, reassuring, and strong as a rock at that moment when I proved to be weak. Looking back I am certainly not surprised, but I digress as it was truly a sign of times to come with her steadiness and undying love. As I write this so many years later, those same tears again trickle down my cheeks, loving the opportunity to relive and thank God for such a wonderful partner in this life.

As mentioned, we have recently celebrated our thirty-first wedding anniversary. We did this at Disney World (more to come on my affinity for the most magical place on earth!) along with our entire crew—what better way to celebrate? Thirty-one years in, and Trudi is more beautiful than ever, more understanding than ever, more wise than ever, and believe it or not, more patient than ever! Her pure heart shines through in her kindness, in her actions, in her prayers, and in every aspect of her life. I know more and more with each passing day just how undeserving I am to call her my wife, but I thank God every single day that I own that privilege. Each day before we head off to work, we make it a point to pray together, to pray for each other and our kids and the lives they lead. It is a small thing, but the bond it creates, along with tears that flow on many days, leads me to cherish this brief but intimate time with her each morning.

Detour quickly with me back to our wedding day. It is glaringly evident that we become one purely by the grace and blessings of our Lord. We enjoyed the festivities of the reception, jumped in the limo heading to the airport, had an amazing honeymoon, and then returned home for Christmas and the aforementioned scavenger hunt. Again, my bride is simply amazing, not only to gracefully deal with that scenario but to set forth on the great adventure that we are still living each and every day. Believe me, I'm a handful, and no one knows that better than Trudi! However, from the moment we said "I do," she was ready to start our family. This bride of mine loves babies more than any other person I have ever met, and she was ready to have her own. In fact, I had never even held a baby at this point in my life, and full disclosure, I have only held three at the time of the publishing of this book. Those babies are our very own Lauren, Cam, and Emma. Little did we know that this part of the journey would prove a bit more difficult than we first thought.

And in case you didn't pick it up . . . *I sure do love my wife!*

Chapter 2

THE STAGE IS SET

Did I mention yet just how much my wife loves babies? We all know that opposites tend to attract, and here is yet another example where this is proven to be a worthy statement. If my wife ever approaches you on the street while you are holding your baby, rest assured her intent is pure! She has an innate love for babies beyond anything I have ever experienced. So of course, the moment we said "I do," she was ready for her own. But as I have grown to appreciate many times throughout the years, God's timing does not always line up with our own.

Here we are as mere babies ourselves, embarking on the greatest adventure either of us had ever imagined, but it turned out we would have a little more time with just the two of us than we originally thought—or maybe better said, than Trudi had envisioned and hoped. Once we made the decision (again, that means when I was finally ready), we agreed it was time for our family to grow. However, as the weeks, months, and years passed, we realized that getting pregnant didn't always prove to be an easy process. After a series of disappointments, we decided it was time to seek professional help and explore medical assistance in our journey of growth. Neither of us really knew what this meant, and remember, this was a time when the internet was still considered somewhat unreliable in its content, so we did what any young enterprising couple would do: we simply forged ahead.

Here is where things could have gone sideways. I knew I had twins within the construct of my family, so with the fertilization enhancement medications, what were we setting ourselves up for? I envisioned a litter of babies, but if that was to be the case, then we simply prayed that they would be healthy. As it turns out, a litter was not in our future, but just like that, the pregnancy test came back positive. This was Christmas Eve, so what an amazing gift we received, and what an amazing gift we were able to give our parents on Christmas Day—the gift of hope and joy in all the things to come with a new baby joining our family!

Here's a moment of transparency for you: I was absolutely terrified! What right did I have to become a dad? What did I know about raising a baby? We decided that we would wait and find out what we were having when the baby arrived, so that even added more questions to my near panic-stricken mindset. Of course, I could never let on to my young bride the fear that I was suppressing, but together, through faith and prayer, we knew we would somehow survive.

The first baby in your house is a big deal. I mean a *really* big deal. First, there is the baby's room. This stage is paramount in how you will be judged by your parents, your peers, even your new little one! Thankfully Trudi had a good idea of where she wanted to go with this. Remember, she'd been planning this for most of her life, so the stage was already set in her mind. I'll let you in on a little secret: as a handyman, I am probably the worst walking this earth. I simply did not, and still do not, possess the skills to do anything remotely akin to fixing household things. This includes painting, so when Trudi decided on this nice seafoam green color and the Beatrix Potter/Peter Rabbit theme for our baby's room, I had no choice but to dive in and do my best to make this the room of her dreams. With a few false starts, and working diligently together, we ultimately produced what I still remember in my mind as the best baby room we had ever seen. Our new little loved one would come home to a room full of Peter

THE STAGE IS SET

Rabbit stuffed animals, mobiles, wallpaper borders, and the list goes on. Room done, we were ready!

Beyond the room, there were a couple of other items to consider. Of course, there is the car seat, the playpen, the toy selection, and those baby clothes that are impossibly tiny, and then we added in one more element—our pure-bred Pekingese pup, Skippy. Skippy was a cool little dog and very much a part of our family. We went to the breeder to pick out a pup, and Skippy was the little guy that latched on to my hand when I picked him up. In ways that we were unaware of, he actually helped prepare us for our new little bundle of joy. Needless to say, he was spoiled rotten, and through some almost comical health issues, we learned a lot about staying calm and digging into the root of the issue. It is quite amazing how the Lord uses little things in life to prepare us for all that is to come. Let me be clear, I am not saying that having a puppy fully prepares you for having kids, but if indeed you are the parent of a fur baby, then you get it!

Having kids is not for the faint of heart. It is the most challenging, most difficult, most tiring, most amazing, most rewarding, and most thrilling ride you will ever embark on. If there is a constant in raising children, it is the old adage that the only constant is indeed *change*! We will walk through some of the stages of change and growth of our kids in the pages to come, and let it be known that everyone's story is not only unique but quite simply just their very own. Knowing that adaptability is a required characteristic of being a dad, a husband, a friend, a provider, and any other title associated with raising kids, also be aware that a decisive mindset is something that you must develop. Flexibility is required, but hear me now when I say this: never be afraid to forge your own path, to do what you feel is the right thing, to take the road less traveled. Trudi and I did this in a multitude of areas in our lives, but the key was that we did it together. And guess what, we still do!

And with that, the stage is set . . . .

Chapter 3

IT'S A GIRL!

"Dad, I'm moving to Florida!"
Proverbs 22:6 tells us, "Train up a child in the way he should go and when he is old he will not depart from it." Trudi and I believe this verse and have lived it with our kids their entire lives, but until they get older and actually live their lives more independently, it is difficult to fully appreciate the impact. We'll get back to Florida, but first let's look back to that wonderful day in August of 1997, the day we first met Lauren.

Trudi's pregnancy with our first child could be classified as "normal." After our difficulties in getting pregnant, there was some angst. *Will the baby be healthy? How many babies would there be? Do we find out what we are having? Wait, are we even prepared to be parents?!* But all in all, the pregnancy went as planned, and Trudi was a beautiful mom-to-be in every facet imaginable. We had decided not to find out what we were having, so after a couple of false starts with labor, the time was finally here.

When I met Lauren Elizabeth Presley for the first time, it changed my life forever. Remember, I had never held a baby before, but when the nurse put her in my arms, life as I knew it shifted and has never been the same since. People say all babies are cute, and I'm not sure I necessarily agree with that, but this tiny baby girl in my arms was the most beautiful thing I had ever seen. This wrinkly, wiggly, beautiful, tiny little human baby girl was indeed mine, and I was immediately hooked. At eight pounds, six ounces, she was not tiny by some comparisons, but her fragility and dependence on us at that moment was galvanizing in a way I still simply cannot express. The life of this little girl was in our hands, and as we fully dedicated her to the Lord, everything we thought had mattered in the past had now changed.

We took Lauren home to her overly decorated Peter Rabbit nursery, and the fun began. I'm almost embarrassed at the amount of video footage that exists of Lauren in her early years—quite literally footage of her doing absolutely nothing that for whatever reason we felt compelled to document. I would say that Trudi did most of the documenting while I was at work each day, but I might get in trouble for that, so we will just leave that right there.

When our family grew again, and then again, we found the amount of footage and pictures diminished in an almost equally embarrassing manner, but we'll save that for later. Yes, there were many sleepless nights, lots of uncertainties, questions we didn't know how to answer, and yes, lots of diapers to be changed. I'll go on the record right here that I was the epitome of a great partner to my bride in shouldering the load on all of these things. Sorry, I can't even write that with a straight face, as it is nowhere close to the real story. Well, I guess that could be a bit of revisionist history. Trudi did all the heavy lifting on those long nights and with all the dirty diapers, and she never once complained about any of it. She was born to be a mom, and *wow*, what a mom she was and still is to this day.

As Lauren grew, little did I know that she would quite literally become a little female version of me. She was, and still is, Daddy's girl. Before she was born I had read Robert Wolgemuth's *She Calls Me Daddy*, and to this day I attribute many of my parenting wins to him and that book. I highly recommend you read this if you are expecting a baby girl. I gave away my original copy to a friend, but I still have a copy in my own personal library today. Anyway, Lauren and I began to do things just for us, and I will revisit these times a bit later in this book. Stay tuned for that.

I remember Lauren's dance recitals. Long, tedious dance recitals. Hours on end of people I didn't know and their kids doing some semblance of performance on a stage in a dark convention center. Did I mention how long these recitals were? But when my baby girl hit the stage, it was a proud dad moment every single time! I remember one year in particular, she was a blue crayon—yes, you read that right. Head to toe a blue crayon, and the words to the accompanying song still resonate in my mind:

> ♪ *I won't grow up*
> *I won't grow up*
> *I don't wanna go to school*
> *I don't wanna go to school*
> *Just learn to be a parrot*
> *And recite the silly rules* ♪

I kid you not! And at the end of *every* show, the grand finale:

> ♪ *It's not how you start it's how you finish* ♪

Every single show! Couple these recitals with the annual Daddy-Daughter dances at school and banquets at church, and my love, admiration, and pride in my baby girl just grew exponentially. You know what, even today that still rings true.

Then there was the time in third grade when, much to our surprise, Lauren wanted to participate in the school talent show and showcase her newly developing piano skills. This was just short of shocking to us as Lauren, in her formative years, tended to be shy, not looking to be in the spotlight in any way. But she wanted to do this, and despite our reservations about whether or not she was ready, we encouraged her to push forward. I'd love to say she nailed that and received a standing ovation from the crowd of her peers and their parents. However, the reality was just a bit different. She started just fine, playing her own rendition of "Amazing Grace," but then it happened. She hit a snag and couldn't recover. So she sat there. Just sat there. Then she attempted to recover, and she should have just sat there. But in the end, she found her way to the finish line. She stood up and fast-walked to her teacher's side on the bleachers, and as soon as she sat down, she burst into tears. Now let me tell you, when you see your baby girl devastated in that manner, it just does something to you. I only remember a couple of other times in her life to this point (she's now twenty-six) when I witnessed this kind of devastation with her, and it quite literally broke my heart. It just speaks to the depth of your love for your children, and while we tried to teach them to clear their own path in life, those are the times when everyone else needs to just get out of the way because my baby needs me and I am on my way!

Of course, Lauren recovered from the trauma of the infamous talent show and grew to become a beautiful and confident young woman. Tennis played a big part in the development of her confidence. In fact, that sport brought about the full development of the attitude that she carries with her to this day. In my eyes, that is a great thing; it taught her to stand up for herself, to be bold, and to believe in herself. Her mom might differ a bit on the value of that same attitude, but we will save that for another time. Lauren's high school tennis career was incredible. I am still convinced she had the best backhand throughout all of our region, and she used it with her doubles partner to own the number one doubles spot through much of her high school time. They experienced great success as a doubles team and also as a full team, reaching the TSSAA state championship round her senior year. They lost that round, placing second in the state, but have I told you just how proud I was of her? I remember her final match at State that year, when they lost to a doubles team they had beaten earlier in the year. It was another one of those devastating moments, but I hurried on the court, and to this day that is still one of my favorite hugs with Lauren. Just to comfort her, to be there for her, to love her. That is the essence of being her dad.

Boys and college. Those are interesting topics. For most of the selection process, Lauren definitely was against going to college close to home. Trudi and I had both attended Union University, right here in the hometown where we live, situated only about five miles from our house. That was out of the question for Lauren. It was all about getting a couple of hours away and experiencing the big SEC school life. But they say God sometimes laughs at our plans, and I firmly believe that.

Late in her senior year of high school, she came to us and told us that she felt like she was supposed to go to Union. We were thrilled but also scared because this is a *very* expensive university, and we were getting a *very* late start in the game. It all came together as God's plans typically do, and Lauren was Union-bound. Trudi and I were so incredibly happy that our firstborn was following our footsteps and attending our alma mater. Lauren would go on to an incredibly successful college career, pledging the same sorority that Trudi had been in at that very school—what a cool connection for them! COVID interrupted Lauren's last year in college, effectively disrupting the "normal" wrap-up of her college path, but even through that, she was able to have a full graduation celebrating her success and awarding her a degree in public relations. The world awaits!

Did I mention boys? That is always a tough topic for dads . . . for many reasons. Simply put, nobody is good enough for our little girls, but we know that God is way out in front of this for us. Lauren was never boy crazy, and for that I am thankful. She dated very little through high school and had one serious relationship in college, but we all know that in God's time, He will allow Lauren and her future husband to meet and fall in love, and that story will be one for the ages, worth telling for generations to come. I'm guessing there might just be another book in the works around that topic for my girls. Only time will tell.

Back to that opening line about moving to Florida. These are words that still grip my heart. When Lauren sets her mind to something, there is no turning back. She told us that she and a couple of friends had decided to get jobs at the beach and move there. At first we thought she was simply pontificating, but she began to actually plan this, and after a couple of months she told us she had found a job. That is when it got real—she was going to move away from us. Some parents live for the day when the kids are all out of the house, but that is not us. At the time of writing this book, Lauren has lived at the beach for a little over two years, serving as a director of client experience at a local wedding and photography business, essentially living her best life. There is not a day that passes that Trudi and I don't miss her desperately, but we are so proud of her boldness to make that move and are thrilled that she is happy and thriving and loving life in general.

I think it is safe to say that with Lauren, she never really wanted to lead. As she grew up, she was content in the background. The girliest of girls with tea parties and baby dolls, yet fierce in her own way. She taught me something about leadership, though. Simply put, I learned from Lauren that it is OK not to lead; rather, there are those who excel in how they follow. That was Lauren. She didn't mindlessly follow the crowd or do things *because everybody else is doing it*. No. She was and still is uniquely her own person. I have watched her evolve as a leader and young woman as she has grown up, and today I do see her actually taking the lead. All those years of following in the right way seemed to have taught her, in some ways, how to actually lead. Leadership comes in many packages, and when your children discover how to unwrap that package in their own lives when they blossom into their own version of how they lead, what a wonderful revelation in their lives and in the lives of us who love them so dearly.

Another caveat where Lauren forged a new path was in preparing me to be the dad for Cam and Emma. I made mistakes with Lauren that could have broken a lesser person, but Lauren was and is a rock, she is confident in who she is, she knows what she wants in life, and in time, God willing, she will find each and every one of those things. She allowed me to experiment on being a dad, whether she was a willing or even witting participant in those experiments or not, but her brother and sister should forever be grateful to her for helping me iron out the wrinkles of my path toward being a better dad.

For Christmas of 2023, Lauren gave me a gift that I'll never be able to put a value on. And no, it wasn't actually her gift to me, although Lauren is an incredibly thoughtful gift giver. No, it was the letter she wrote to Trudi and me. In this letter she told Trudi that over the years she has learned to appreciate her love and abject selflessness more and more. How Trudi loves Lauren (and all of us for that matter) is unmatched and that is a clear beacon to Lauren now that she is getting older. She went on to tell me in this letter that the older she gets, the more she realizes just how much like me she is. I'm not sure I would wish that on anyone, but her next sentence is what really got me. She stated that while she knows she is just like me, there is no one else in the world that she would want to be like. I cried when I read that for the first time, and admittedly it brings tears to my eyes as I write it even now. Those words from our firstborn make both of us so proud, and we are indeed thankful for her and the young woman she has become.

I grew up *with* her as a dad to Lauren. As our first-born, we didn't know what we were doing. And I most certainly didn't know how to be a dad. All I ever wanted was to be there for her, to teach her, to comfort her, to provide for her, and ultimately to love her. Twenty-six years later I am still growing as a dad, but it is my hope that as Lauren continues to grow as a young woman, she will always know just how special she is, how much I love and adore her, how much she changed me for the better, and of course, how proud I am of her.

And by the way . . . *I sure do love my girl!*

Chapter 4

IT'S A BOY!

"Dad, we're getting married!" March 13, 2000. We were a couple of months beyond the delusional scares that the new millennium was supposed to usher in, so life was back to normal. Lauren was now settled in as a rambunctious two-and-a-half-year-old, and baby number two was on the way. This time we didn't have the difficulties getting pregnant as we did with Lauren. In fact, quite the opposite as about the moment we decided it was time to try for number two . . . *What, you're pregnant?! That was fast!* But we were thrilled, and this time we wanted to know ahead of time what we were having. We could not have been more thrilled when that ultrasound showed us that baby number two would indeed be a boy. Like most dads, I swelled with pride thinking over all of the amazing adventures I would have with my little boy. But before we could begin traversing that path, we had to face a difficult situation.

Mr. Charlie was Trudi's dad, my father-in-law. He was such an amazing man, and we will talk more about him in a later chapter. But part of his story fits right here with our son. Mr. Charlie had battled non-Hodgkin's lymphoma, a form of cancer, for some time now, but for the last few weeks of his life, he was hospitalized and spent his days in his hospital bed. I knew one thing for sure: he was determined to meet his newest grandson. On the day that our son Cameron Thomas Presley was born, Mr. Charlie was wheeled down to Trudi's hospital room—yes, in the very same hospital—to hold his grandson. He beamed with pride as he held this little eight pound, fourteen ounce bundle of energy, and he, like all of us, loved him deeply. It was just over a month later that the Lord called Mr. Charlie home, but he proved the power of the human spirit by hanging on, in my humble opinion, just to meet our baby boy, Cam. He may not have been present physically to enjoy Cam's prowess on the athletic field, but I know for a fact that he had the best seat in the house as he watched him grow and enjoy the sports he played.

Cam was a fat baby and measured off the charts in nearly every measurable category at our pediatrician visits. As he grew, some of those measurables calmed down a bit, but at an early age, we could see his wit and character developing. At the age of two, Cam had to get glasses. That was an incredibly traumatic event for us as his parents, but I remember his ophthalmologist reminding us that this was not a catastrophic event but simply that our son needed corrective eyewear. He took to his glasses beautifully and would eventually outgrow the accommodative issue with his eyes, thus dropping the need for them and continuing on his path as a rambunctious little boy.

Along these same lines, I want to include a bit about our pediatrician. This actually applies to all three of our kids, but since Cam is the main character in this particular chapter, this seemed to be the right spot for insertion. Every family needs a go-to pediatrician. We were blessed to have Dr. Scott Owens in our lives for Lauren, Cam, and Emma. Dr. Owens has since gone to be with the Lord, but we were blessed beyond measure that he was in our lives as our kids grew up. He had a wonderful calm demeanor, something all parents, but particularly new ones, need in their lives. When we might be on the verge of a meltdown, he would simply reassure us that whatever we were experiencing was normal and that this too shall pass. He was a godly man whose faith was evident, and I firmly believe that God put him in our lives at just the right time to care for our kids.

Now, thankfully Dr. Owens had a sense of humor too. Cam was about three years old and in for a checkup. After the normal check-

IT'S A BOY!

in and waiting process, we were sitting back in an exam room again *waiting* to see the doctor. Did I mention that Cam was a normal, rambunctious little boy? Well, he also had, and still has, quite the wit and sense of humor about him. Cam decided it was appropriate to take off his clothes and climb up on the exam table facing the wall. As Dr. Owens entered the room, Cam proceeded to greet him by placing his hands on his butt cheeks and, by moving said cheeks, mimed, "Hello, Dr. Owens" while comically stating the accompanying words. Trudi was mortified, I was on the floor laughing, and Cam was business as usual. I'm confident Dr. Owens never again received a greeting quite like that and possibly never recovered from it, but it was a moment that went down in the Presley household lore as something we would never forget. Gotta love that kid!

As Cam grew, it became evident that he was blessed with a beautiful combination of Trudi's intellect and my "street smarts" (thank goodness those were not reversed), both of which would serve him well in life. He also showed a certain amount of prowess in athletics. He started with t-ball and church league basketball at around four years old. Over the years, whatever company I happened to work for at the time would invariably find its way onto the jersey of Cam's baseball team as the sponsor, and if you know me, there were quite a few variations of those along the way!

Cam became an accomplished shortstop in baseball with a cannon for an arm. He was emerging as an outstanding quarterback and defensive back in football through his middle school years and was a defensive beast playing the three spot on the basketball court. More time was devoted to baseball than the other sports, as we developed a travel team called the Vipers. The stories of our travel ball days could be another book completely, but suffice it to say it was an amazing time in our lives! What a joy it was traveling around the south playing in tournaments, dragging his siblings along for the ride. Those days of travel ball will always hold a special place with me, and if the truth is to be told, that was Trudi's favorite sport of all.

But around the time Cam entered high school, the game of baseball slowed down for him, football didn't resonate with him, and basketball was proving to be incredibly physical, leading to multiple injuries. What really shifted in Cam's sports journey was watching

DEVELOPING DAD

Lauren play tennis at the TSSAA state championships when he was in eighth grade. He looked around at the people playing, watched the sport itself, and realized he could be special in this sport. Considering the fact that he had never held a racket at this point aside, he made the decision to become a tennis player. He stopped baseball and football immediately and played only one more season of basketball, all the while devoting himself completely to developing his tennis game.

This proved to be a pivotal decision in his life and a good one at that! He practiced hours on end each day, hitting thousands of balls and playing tournaments all around the southeast. It was rigorous, but I loved every minute of it. Tennis sometimes brought out the worst in Cam, and we have a display wall full of smashed rackets to prove it (Trudi despises this by the way), numbering well into double digits of destroyed equipment along the way. But he continued to develop and became an incredible player, winning two TSSAA state championships and receiving twenty-three collegiate offers to play as well. Cam and Lauren teamed up in mixed doubles to win the local city tournament a couple of times, and it was so much fun watching them compete together! Side note, did I mention that Cam got the best of both worlds from me and Trudi? His academic offers came in as well, and ultimately he opted not to play college tennis and move on to be a college kid. Little did he know, this would lead to the most amazing blessing in his life.

Stepping back, throughout high school, Cam didn't date very much but did have a relationship through a good part of his senior year. At this point, he was incredibly focused on the development of and success on the tennis court, so that was his primary area of concern. That focus drove his college selection choice early on, leading him to sign to play at a D2 college in southern Mississippi. Through the completion of his senior year and his aforementioned accomplishments on the court, Cam began to realize that tennis might not need to be his driving force behind where to continue his education. Ultimately he opted not to pursue tennis any further, what again proved to be a God-ordained decision as his college journey continued.

Cam went on to college and, through an incredibly cool series of circumstances, pledged the same chapter of the same fraternity

IT'S A BOY!

at the same university where I had done all of the above. We bonded in a way that is quite uncommon with this, and it will be something I will always cherish as well. He went on to be one of the youngest brothers elected as president of our fraternity, and then he served two consecutive terms, growing as a leader throughout the process. Intramural sports scratched the itch for continued athletic competition, and Cam loved his college years. But wait, that isn't the most important part of this story.

Back in the spring of Cam's senior year of high school, Lauren was in college and hosted a high school senior for the Presidential Scholars of Excellence competition at Union University. This is where incoming freshmen who have achieved the highest academic standards compete for the big scholarship money. Cam qualified, was invited, and participated in this elite competition as well but on a different weekend from when Lauren hosted this young girl from Lee's Summit, MO. Her name was Glori, and Lauren called Cam to tell him that she was hosting the girl that he needed to marry! Cam had not yet even met Glori, but suffice it to say that at the time of the writing of this book, I am thrilled to introduce you to Mr. and Mrs. Presley. We couldn't be happier for them and can't wait to follow the story of their new life together and see just how the Lord blesses them.

The opening line of this chapter encompasses the culmination of so many wonderful things that Cam has brought into our lives. He is a joy to be around, with a quick wit and beautiful intellect. He has Trudi's heart, as he looks to take care of others in a very unselfish way, a trait I certainly wish I had more of in my own life. His loyalty is unmatched, yet another trait that I am proud of as his dad. I often find myself reflecting on the life he has led to this point, wondering just where the Lord will lead him. As Trudi and my marriage has grown over these last thirty-one years, our prayer is that we have modeled for him a marriage that encapsulates faith, compromise, unselfishness, and love that he can emulate and even improve on in his own marriage. As I write this, I think back to the toast to Cam and Glori that I gave, along with family and friends, and the emotions that awaken in me are real to this very day.

Cam is my little boy. He may stand six feet two compared to my five feet ten, but he will always be my little boy. As I pray he looks up to me as a role model and a dad, I literally look up to him in stature, but more importantly for the man he is becoming. I'll never forget him running around the house in his superhero outfits, truly believing he was Superman, Spiderman, or the Flash, and loving every minute of it. Cam has always been an unwitting leader, someone whom others intrinsically follow whether he is purposefully leading or not. He is on a journey well traveled so far, and I am confident that adventure will continue as such.

Cam graduated from college in the spring semester with his athletic training degree and has begun to work for a time in that field, dedicating himself to helping ensure the safety of high school athletes. His career path can lead anywhere he wants, so no matter what that may look like down the road, I am confident he will continue helping countless people along that path. A truly noble calling and one that is a perfect fit for the man he is becoming.

The Wedding

In June of 2023, we gained a new daughter. Technically a daughter-in-law, but we love Glori like she has always been our own. Let me tell you why we love her this way. Yes, she is beautiful, smart, courteous, and driven—all qualities that any parent would love in the forever partner of their child. Glori loves the Lord and brings something new to our family—a midwestern twist (she's from Lee's Summit just outside of Kansas City, MO). There are funny conversations that take place when the vernacular we are accustomed to clashes with hers. For example, we lived in a *cove* at one time, but to Glori that would be a *cul-de-sac*. When we go to the store, we grab a *buggy*, whereas she grabs a *cart*. We laugh about these things and wonder how in the world those types of nuances ever even began! But while all of that plays into the easy acceptance of Glori into our family, here is the kicker: she loves our boy! Genuinely, wholly, unequivocally—she loves Cam, and for that very reason, she will forever be one of us.

Their wedding was one for the ages. Admittedly I have not been to many weddings in my life. Aside from my own, maybe a

IT'S A BOY!

handful, tops. Weddings today are quite different from back in our time, but it was a fun process and the final result was spectacular. They chose a venue a couple of hours away from our home, and it was a beautiful setting. All of the work, all of the stress, all of the money—everything that went into the prep for the day was well worth it. The rehearsal dinner was splendid, and I may or may not have cried while delivering my toast to the bride and groom. It was so enlightening to listen to their friends and family tell stories about Cam and Glori's life together over the four years leading to this point. They are truly blessed and loved by this group of people, and as a dad, my heart was full.

Wedding day arrives in June, but remember this is summer in the south! However, the Lord blessed them with the most amazing day. The temperature was perfect for the shaded outdoor area they had chosen to exchange vows. Trudi and I watched as the processional came together and formed the wedding party at the front. In all of my years watching Cam excel in almost every aspect of his life, I had never been more proud as I watched him anticipate his first glimpse of Glori coming down the aisle. When he did see her, the waterworks began. The look on his face still brings tears to my eyes as he begins to cry himself. I know this feeling personally as it was the exact same experience for me when I first saw Trudi approaching me more than thirty years ago. The minister reached out to Cam in support, and I watched as his best man began to cry as well. At that point, it was over for me. I'm pretty sure I cried more than Trudi, more than Cam, more than anyone in the wedding party, and I am not ashamed. Those tears were tears of sheer joy and pride. I've never been happier for my baby boy.

The ceremony was something from a storybook, followed by a perfect reception. Later, as they exited to begin their honeymoon journey, I held Trudi and we cried once again. This may sound odd as I write this book, but I was, and really still am, speechless when it comes to being able to express how perfect that day was. And it remains my prayer that indeed that was only the beginning, and that Cam and Glori will live a lifetime of adventure, joy, success, and happiness, always keeping the Lord at the center of their marriage.

I see so many things in Cam that remind me of a younger me, and part of that thrills me while some of it terrifies me. To this day, I think back to his days on the tennis court, and they are memories I will always cherish. When I have the opportunity to speak for groups of people, I still tell stories of those days and the obstacles he had to overcome along his path to success. All of that helped mold him and teach him valuable lessons about wins and losses, character, persistence, leadership, and the value of good old-fashioned hard work. I pray that he will lead his life with love and encouragement of others, holding Glori and all things dear to him closer than imaginable, and that indeed he goes on to truly have a positive impact in ways we have only begun to imagine.

And in case you're wondering . . . *I sure do love my boy!*

Chapter 5

IT'S A(*NOTHER*) GIRL!

"Dad, we did it! We won!"
Have you ever been asked a question seemingly so strange that it just leaves you dumbfounded? It is New Year's Eve, and we are at the hospital for the delivery of baby number three. As with Lauren and Cam, we get all settled in, and at the appointed time, Trudi receives her epidural. Usually, at this point, time sort of slows down, so I do what every good husband does—I tell my wife I'm going downstairs to get a burger while we wait. I know, husband of the year material, right? The mother/baby unit at our hospital is on the third floor, and the food court is in the basement. I'm in line, waiting to order, and I feel a tap on my shoulder. I turn around and look down, and there stands my mom. She simply said, "She's pushing!" If there was a record for ascending the four flights of stairs from the basement to the third floor previously, I shattered it, and I am pretty confident my new record still stands today!

I enter the room, and sure enough, the doctor is there, and our family is about to grow yet again. As the baby is delivered though, Dr. Rogers looks up at me and asks this question: "Have any of your other kids been born with an extra appendage?" I don't know about you, but even though I clearly knew the answer to her question, I was rendered speechless for a moment, with every worst-case scenario rushing through my mind.

For our third child, we found out beforehand that we would be blessed with another girl. I'll admit that as my girls get older, I think of that blessing at times with dollar signs behind them because of future weddings and the like . . . but I digress. When Emma Grace Presley graced us with her presence, albeit over a week late, she brought with her a little extra surprise. Attached to her hand was a small skin tag. I say small because at nine pounds, one ounce, not much else was small about her upon arrival. This tag was an odd shape, almost like a ball attached to a string. It was on the side of her hand, so at any given time before she was born, she could have been holding that ball or playing with it! After the shock of Dr. Roger's question and the determination that no, in fact, none of our other kids brought any extra luggage with them, we asked what to do about it. It was a simple procedure to tie it off, leaving a small scar that should never be an issue. That has indeed proven to be the fact, but it still remains a bit of a rude awakening to be asked such a question before you ever lay eyes on your new baby. Needless to say, baby Emma was perfect, even with the extra baggage she brought with her.

I grew up with one sister. Trudi grew up with two brothers. Both of these scenarios seemed completely normal to each of us. After Cam was born, I sort of assumed that our family was complete. If you recall, however, I mentioned earlier that Trudi loves babies, and whether she would ever admit it or not, I think she was planning for more all along! I'm not saying she was sneaky or anything, but I do recall that sunny spring afternoon when she walked out of the bathroom holding that little stick, quietly mouthing the words, "I'm pregnant!" Cam was not quite yet three years old, and Lauren was just over six, and we had not even discussed trying to have another baby just yet. But as we all know and I have previously stated, at times God laughs at man's plans. What initially rendered me in a bit of shock quickly transformed into pure joy—we were going to have another baby!

As time flew by, we were fast approaching Trudi's due date, determined ahead of time to be the day after Christmas. But that

IT'S A(NOTHER) GIRL!

day came and went, and still no Emma. So on what became daily follow-up visits with the doctor, December 30th rolled around, and we were still waiting. I remember asking the doctor if there was any risk or potential harm to either Trudi or the baby if we induced, and I was met with the cynical response, "Oh, so you are hoping to gain another tax write-off this year, huh?" Well no, that was not my intent, but since you mentioned it, why not? Of course, there was no inherent risk at that point, so we went home and returned to the hospital on December 31st. Emma was born soon after our arrival, and she immediately became the recipient of a perpetual party to be held in her honor every single December 31st going forward. It was a long time before we told her that those fireworks and parties also coincided with the celebration of ringing in the New Year, but that is just semantics.

I often tell people that if three kids can be opposites, then ours have accomplished that. While Emma was nearly the spitting image of Lauren as a baby and through her younger years, they were, and still remain, very different people. Even today there is no mistaking that they are sisters, and as Emma grows and matures, I even see more and more similarities in them than in the formative years. As the third child, let's just get some of the facts out there and own them. First, I'm still not convinced that her calling is not to be an attorney, because she can surely argue with the best of them. That said, she is now an accounting major, and I think without a doubt she will be the best accountant in her field.

Remember when I told you we had endless hours of footage of Lauren, basically even when she was doing absolutely nothing? That trend continued somewhat with Cam, and the two of them together. But, maybe not so much with baby number three. Looking back I'm still not sure if Emma was even in our house for a good part of her early days, at least there doesn't seem to be much video or picture proof of it. Lauren has this amazing, detailed baby book with everything you can possibly imagine included therein. Cam has a book as well, albeit not to the point of completion or detail of Lauren's. Then, Emma has a book . . . period. That's about all I can say about it!

Now don't get me wrong, our love for Emma is as genuine and true as it is for Lauren and Cam. But it is a good thing she knows that because if she needs visual proof of that love, then she might be out of luck. She really does take this in a good-natured spirit, but every now and then she has to take her shot at us about that, and who could blame her?

Emma's early years were a bit different than Lauren's in many ways. Emma had the good fortune of Trudi and I learning from our mistakes we made on both Lauren and Cam. I'm not sure if that was really good or bad for her, but I will go ahead and tell you now that she turned out pretty amazing, if I do say so myself! She also had the privilege of being exposed to the world of travel baseball and all the activities and events of her older siblings. All the while though, whether she or we realized it or not, she was formulating her own way, her own mindset, and her own path that she would follow.

Enter the world of competitive cheer. I'll be the first to admit that I had never seen myself as a "cheer dad." I conjured up images of wild, obnoxious, over-the-top dads who were more interested in drawing attention to themselves than to their own child and their competition. And time would prove me to be right on many occasions with that assessment. But that said, I've always told my kids that I wanted them simply to be passionate about something, and I would love and support that passion along with them. That turned out to be cheer for Emma.

All total, she competed in this field for eight years. We traveled all over the southeast to some really great venues and some really awful ones. There were so many random hotel stays and meals on the run that we can't count them to this day. Admittedly another area we can't count, or at least choose not to, is the money we spent along the way—but I won't dive too deep into that part. Over time, Emma began to really excel in cheer, in every aspect of it. As an eventual Level 5 tumbler, I was blown away by the skill and athletic ability she exhibited. With seeming springs in her legs, the way she could soar around that stage was astounding! She grew incredibly strong physically as well as developed beautiful rhythm to boot, and she sure did shine on stage in her performances. Thinking back through all of those competitions, I am proud to say I can't recall a single slip, fall, drop, or mishap that could be attributed to Emma's fault, and that in and of itself is an amazing feat.

But there was more, much more to this time in her life. Through this showy competitive field, I watched Emma emerge from an incredibly quiet and introverted child to a bold and confident young woman. Even more, I saw her emerge as a leader among her peers, not vocally as I so often witnessed in these groups, but with her actions. Her commitment and dedication, her desire for excellence and to win, indeed her very leadership ability blossomed through this time in her life, and I simply cannot put a value on how important that remains in her life today. She and her team won countless competitions, including CheerSport, the largest competition of its kind in the world, along with the international championships at Disney, yes the same event you have seen most likely on ESPN! She would say her biggest accomplishment to date was winning at CheerSport, thus the opening line of this chapter, but I have a feeling there will be so many more victories along the way that she hasn't even begun to imagine. Of course, there were losses along the way, but through it all, Emma led with dignity and pride, and her growth in every aspect of her life was phenomenal.

Leadership is something that is near and dear to my heart. We've discussed how early in life Lauren was a beautiful follower and how I have seen her evolve into her own style of strong leadership. Cam was born a leader, and it just took a little time for him to embrace that. No surprise, Emma's leadership style is different from either of them. One would not peg Emma as a leader. She has a quiet demeanor and is comfortable being behind the scenes. But her cheer days showed a side of her leadership where it was simply this: she chose to lead by example. The first one in and the last one out. Not vocal, not even necessarily in the spotlight, and maybe more importantly, not even wanting the spotlight. Leadership has many faces, and I am so proud to see how each of our kids developed their own style and methodology in order to impact the lives of others.

Mixed in with Emma's cheer prowess was the sport I've already mentioned with Lauren and Cam: tennis. As we have discussed, both Lauren and Cam found their niche in this realm. Not their identity per se, but certainly their passion. It only made sense that Emma made her run in this sport as well. She started her freshman year in high school, and it was evident from the onset that she could be special in this sport as well if she chose that path. Well, that was not to be. Don't get me wrong, her talent was unmistakable, but her heart was just not in it. I love the fact that she played, and I will never be convinced that she did that for any reason other than for me. She quickly rose through the high school ranks at her school and her junior year had some phenomenal match wins and big advancements both physically and mentally in the game. But still, her heart wasn't in it. She and I sat down before the season of her senior year, and I basically convinced her not to play that year. I wanted her senior year to be excellent on all fronts, and while she would have certainly helped us on the team, I wanted her focus and passion to be solely where *she* wanted it, and that was cheer. It was the right decision and one neither she nor I will ever regret.

Unlike Lauren and Cam, Emma knew early on that she wanted to go to Union University like the rest of the family did for college. Trudi and I thought she should be able to go for free since she would be the fifth from the Presley family to attend there, but no such luck. However, did I mention that she is her mother's child? That intellect and intelligence, combined with her years of leadership and confidence development through cheer, won her fantastic scholarships, and she was all set! She moved into the dorms as a freshman and immediately followed in the footsteps of both Trudi and Lauren, pledging their sorority. She was off and running! At the time of my writing this book, she is a declared accounting major, and I'm willing to bet the house that she will excel on this front as she has in all others.

Fast-forward to the back end of Emma's sophomore year of college. I've watched her through some ups and downs so far in college life. She came out of the gate fast and morphed into an incredible version of herself that I loved seeing. Being bold, putting herself out there, and truly coming into this new and wonderful version of herself. Over the last year, I watched her lose some of that momentum for no apparent reason, so I encourage her on a regular basis to be confident in the beautiful young woman that she is and put herself out there. Time will tell how her college career will continue to evolve, but I am confident in her and the tenacious side she possesses and the great outcomes that will follow. As I pen these words, she has already regained that early traction and is once again shining in the way that only she can.

Oh, and boys must be discussed as well. Emma chose not to date much through high school, but starting in college she is enjoying meeting new people and going to her own sorority parties as well as the fraternity parties with different people. Largely to avoid the "double-function-assumption" of social life at a relatively small college but also to continue to meet new people and explore the plan that God has for her.

Emma is certainly her own person, and I would not have it any other way. I love how deeply loyal she is and how her passion shines through in the things she believes in. All three of our kids have the ability to sing, but Emma is the only one I have ever heard much from on this front. I will text her from time to time and tell her how much I miss our times of carpool karaoke. If you are not familiar with that term, we have a playlist of songs that we sing together, harmonizing and singing both our individual parts as well as the combined efforts included in such duets. Emma has incredible talent in this area, although I'm not sure she will ever share it with anyone outside of the confines of our car sessions. Her harmony is spot on, and her range is quite amazing. My voice never was anything to write home about, but I can carry a tune. Like in most things, we are all better together, so singing along with Emma makes me feel like I can actually still perform. But the real joy comes from watching her out of the corner of my eye as she effortlessly navigates the harmony and notes of some of our favorite songs. This will forever remain a favorite between me and my youngest baby girl.

Since the time she was very young, she has watched Lauren and Cam closely. Our kids are not overly vocal about their affection for each other, but I see it in all of them. Emma again exhibits that fierce loyalty to them, and that is a trait that I pray never fades. I cannot wait to see how she continues to develop and evolve as a young woman through college and beyond, and I know that she is bound for greatness in whatever she chooses to pursue. Oh, and by the way, circling back to my opening statement . . . Emma and her team did win the largest cheer competition in the world! I will forever cherish that moment when her victory was announced—the pure undulating joy she exuded and the pride of a job so very well done! And that hug afterward, that's the stuff of legends!

And just in case you missed it . . . *I sure do love my girl!*

Chapter 6

BEFORE...

Before I was a husband, I was a son.

As we are traveling through the desert of Arizona, I am oblivious to much going on around me. Like any six-year-old boy, I was just happy to be there. At that time in my life, my dad drove an eighteen-wheeler for the United States Post Office, and I was riding on the "doghouse" between my dad and his driving partner, Mr. Percy. My dad typically left on Sunday afternoon and would return the following Saturday, so at that point in my life we didn't see him very much. In fact, my mom was the person who taught me to kick a football, and that in and of itself is probably why I never made it as a punter! You have to give her credit for trying though. She was a beautiful soul and one of the very best women I ever knew, and I loved her dearly . . . but she was no athlete. Anyway, back to Arizona.

We are traveling along, not far from the California border, when we hit an air pocket. This is a strange phenomenon to this day for me to comprehend, but it happened and was traumatic enough for me to recall it all these years later. When our rig hit this air pocket, it blew out the passenger side windshield of my dad's truck which hit him square in the face. I don't recall all of the details of that particular moment, but I remember the damage to his face, his loss of consciousness, and Mr. Percy grabbing me and holding me tight as I had an absolute fit, wanting to help my dad. It was no small miracle that I was not injured as well, considering I was leaning over on my dad's shoulder at that time—at least that is how Mr. Percy relayed it to me later.

Fast-forward a few days, and my dad has his first round of surgeries completed. He is conscious and almost ready to be transported back home. I have no recollection of how we got home, but the vision of that windshield hitting him, Mr. Percy corralling me, and looking into the sleeper of the rig to see my favorite stuffed animal crushed by the windshield as it found its resting spot—all of these are still crystal clear in my mind. Funny how this particular story popped into my mind as I considered my formative years, but there you have it. Needless to say, my dad survived with a few scars to show, as did my stuffed animal "Froggy" who also gained a new scar to boot!

As a son, I was a pretty good kid, if not a bit mischievous. I loved to play outside, fish, ride my bike, and just be a kid. Looking back, I have to admit I was a bit of a nerdy kid, but I didn't know that at the time. I went to a private school through my middle school grades, although I'm not sure I really fit in with the perceived socio-economic status of that school at the time. My parents wanted the best for me and my sister though, so they sacrificed as needed to provide for us. My mom worked for the government, and you're already familiar with a bit of my dad's career (more on him later). We were the typical middle-class family in small-town USA, and life was good.

I'll counter the opening of that last paragraph with a story that could prove otherwise. I don't remember how old I was, but the rest of this story lives in vivid color in my mind as I recount this experience. Let's say I was about eight years old, and my family had made the short trek from Brownsville, TN, over to Jackson, TN. This was a big deal as a kid, as we considered Jackson to be the big city! And of course, any family adventure to Jackson included a visit to K-Mart. Most of you reading this book will have never even heard of K-Mart, but suffice it to say that it was an early predecessor

BEFORE...

to the behemoth we know as Wal-Mart today. They had a deli in the front with the best ham sandwiches known to man alongside a slushie machine with cola and cherry flavors available. In the back, there was an actual sit-down restaurant, but we didn't really have the money for that extravagance growing up, so I would walk by envious of those rich people who could indulge in such luxury. Then there was the excitement when the store manager would hop on the in-store microphone to announce the latest blue-light special. There would be a literal spot designated in the store where they would roll out a cart with a flashing blue light and put items on sale for a few minutes based on that exciting development. It was an experience for sure, and invariably we would rush around the store to find out what unique and exciting items were up for grabs at crazy low prices for the next fifteen minutes!

Yes, K-Mart was great, and they had a little bit of everything, but what I remember most is their fantastic toy department. I remember perusing aisle after aisle of toys, electronics, and games, and the endless assortment of little toy cars. In fact, I loved this area so much that, one fateful evening, I decided a few of these items needed to go home with me. Did I mention I had no money, no chance that my dad would buy them for me, and in my mind, no chance that I would get caught if I made my move? Well, I did just that, I made my move. All these years later I still recall the night I became a thief. And I must say it was quite the haul for my first foray into the underbelly of the criminal realm. Of all the treasures before me, here is what my kid brain decided was worth the risk of petty larceny. I took a molded plastic figure of Rudy, a character from the cartoon series *Fat Albert*, and I stuck him in my pocket. Then, I picked up a green plastic rendition of a motorcycle, and I stuck it under my shirt. Then, to top it off, as we were exiting, I grabbed a pack of gum and slid that in the other pocket of my blue jeans. I was loaded for bear, and my criminal career was underway.

As we approached our 1975 Ford Station Wagon, all green and wood grain siding, I pulled out that green plastic motorcycle and asked an incredibly profound question: *How did this get here?!* Well, let me say that night was not only the beginning of my crime streak, it was also the end. My dad made me go back inside K-Mart alone and find someone to tell what I had done and offer an apology. His mistake was not going with me because not only did I not apologize to anyone, I barely stepped inside the doors of the store, threw that motorcycle just to the right inside the building, and hightailed it right back out to the car. I thought I was home free, but my punishment was forthcoming. We drove a couple miles down the road and stopped in a circle drive of a house right on Old Bells Highway. In fact, I could take you to that very spot today and show you where I learned my lesson on the evils of stealing from K-Mart. My dad used his belt to teach me the error of my ways, and if those people were at home that evening, they got to witness a transformation of epic proportions going down in their front yard!

We proceeded home that evening, with me sniffling in the very back, sideways-facing, flip-up seat of that station wagon, thinking of all the terrible ways that I could get back at my dad for his correction of me and the misstep I had taken that night. But then it hit me. I still had a pack of Juicy Fruit and little Rudy in my pockets! Oh, the retribution that awaited me if my parents found out about the continued egregiousness of my crimes! So I did what any quick-witted eight-year-old boy would do. I kept that part a secret until we got home, feigned an upset stomach, and proceeded to flush both that pack of gum and little Rudy right down the toilet. Problem solved! Thus the beginning and the end of my reign of terror as a criminal. And at this point, as I put this in print, I would hope that the statute of limitations for my crime has elapsed, but K-Mart is now defunct anyway so I guess I will survive further prosecution.

In middle school, I picked up sports by playing football and basketball, and though I'm not sure I was very good at either one, I was able to secure a spot as a starting running back and point guard, respectively. Sports played an impressionable part in my life from that time forward, and I am thankful for that. Entering high school, however, I transferred to the larger public high school in my county. I quickly realized I would not be a starter in any capacity here, and I didn't even want to try. Enter tennis into my life and the beginning, albeit a bit late, of a solid high school career, leading to the opportunity to play small college tennis down the road. My church was a huge part of my life in high school, affording me opportunities to grow as

BEFORE...

a Christian, travel on mission trips to places I had never been, and explore talents I didn't know I had. *Talent* might be a stretch, but I realized I could at least carry a tune, so in addition to tennis and church, singing became a part of my life as well.

My parents were both hard-working, blue-collar types, so their work usually prohibited them from seeing my matches or performances, but I knew how much they loved me anyway. Their work ethic was ingrained into me at an early age, and I started my working career as a stock boy at the local IGA grocery store. I wish I could say that I was a model employee, but I was fourteen years old and still had a lot to learn. I remember my manager, Marvin, a heavy-set affable type who was probably just out of high school himself. Marvin didn't do much to teach me about hard work or leadership, but he did teach me about having fun at work. We may or may not have dumped our mop buckets on the floor of the stock room and took turns running and sliding through the soapy water after we shut the doors on the weekend stock nights. But either way, we eventually dialed in and got our work done and collected those big paychecks in the noble world of stocking shelves and carrying groceries to the trunks of our customers' cars. This was my very first introduction to the world of customer service, the key word being *service*, and this was something I have carried with me to this very day.

Leadership is something I study and strive to constantly improve in my life. In high school, depending on who you asked, I could be seen as a potent force of leadership or simply as some guy in the hall. At school, I had a certain group of friends and did fine, but aside from my tennis experience, I didn't assert myself as a leader very much in that realm. I just didn't have the level of confidence required to push through the silliness and stigmas of high school drama to emerge as much of a leader. My church family was a bit of a different story. Ralph Brown was my youth minister and had as big of an impact on my life as anyone I ever encountered in my formative years. His belief in me gave me the confidence to lead, to try new things, to be bold, and ultimately to emerge and grow as a leader, and he consistently pushed me to grow in Christ as my first priority. I will forever be indebted to Bro. Ralph, and he may never know this side of heaven just how much he impacted me and so many others just like me. I am forever grateful for the influence, guidance, and unconditional love he showed me for those years in my life.

Those aforementioned misses by my parents, the assists from Bro. Ralph, along with an early dive into the world of work, galvanized something within me, and I knew that when the day came that I had my own kids, I would move heaven and earth to be sure I was there for them. If they have ever wondered why I was so determined to be by their side and be a part of their activities, there you have it. I realize that I have embarrassed them on many occasions as they grew up by hugging them, kissing them, and telling them I love them right in front of their friends—yes, even through middle and high school. Even now I still do that in their new phases of life, and I hope they have gained a bit more understanding of just how important it is to me that they always know beyond any doubt just how much I truly love them.

I've said it before, but it is worth repeating: we all just want *better* for our kids than what we had, no matter how good or how bad we had it growing up. These stories and people I've just introduced you to all proved pivotal in the development of my life, which would come to fruition as I grew. An impressionable kid, a shy middle-schooler, a mixed bag in high school, then on to college. Formative years to say the least, and then the introduction to my future bride when it all began to crystalize.

Before I Was a Dad, I Was a Husband

I have had many jobs in my career. In fact, at the time of the publication of this book, I am working in my sixteenth role post-college. Thankfully, my one and only wife (*thank You, Lord, for Trudi*) has stuck with me through all of the change and transition over the years. I'm not sure if my career has served to strengthen me as a husband or make me weak, but I have tried to take away the good and the bad from all of those stops along my path and apply them to be better in my life, specifically in my marriage. I've heard men who are like me and have been married to their high school or college sweetheart jokingly say something like, *Let me introduce you to my first wife.* Coming from someone who has been married to the same woman for thirty-plus years, that introductory line may be somewhat comical, but I've never been bent toward anything like that. To me it gives forth a finite version of the love we share, and I never want to do anything to limit the abounding love we share and the time we get to share it together.

Let's go back to 1992. I remember meeting with our pastor for premarital counseling. One of the things he told us was that we should never go to bed angry with each other and that we should always strive to go to bed at the same time. Nearly thirty-two years later, we still make this our practice. I doubt Trudi remembers that edict from him, but there is something special about starting and ending each day with the one you love, just in a simple ritual of synchronizing our timing around sleep. He also told Trudi that I would test her patience much more over the years than she ever would for me. I was somewhat offended at the young age of twenty-three, particularly since this pastor didn't know me all that well just yet. You know what, that man proved prophetic in his statement! I certainly have my hands full with that guy I see staring back at me in the mirror every day, and I thank God for giving Trudi the patience of Job to handle me as well.

Being a good husband is an intentional effort. Those who know me know quite well that I think I am usually right. Whether or not that proves accurate is up for debate. But Trudi is a completely different story as she is almost *always* right! I will not live that statement down, but the facts are the facts. Her intuition is spot on, and without a doubt, she is blessed with the gift of discernment. I can't count the times when Trudi would offer me counsel, usually about a job opportunity, and I would choose to follow my own path. Too many times to count, I would walk away from a position just knowing that the grass would indeed be greener in my new role. Trudi would warn me, "All of these companies and positions always end up the same," and of course she would be right. "This time" was a phrase I adopted to convince myself that indeed I could change the company to accommodate my need for fulfillment, only to eventually be let down by the leadership of each stop along my way. Today, I would say "next time" has become one of my favorite phrases, not so much because of what the past may hold, but because next time can indeed be used by the Lord to do a great work in me. "Next time" is a powerful thought process if adopted properly and applied in the way God intends.

Here's the thing though: through all of my missteps and, yes, blatant mistakes, not one time has Trudi ever vocalized the words, *I told you so*, even though she could have done so almost every day for the entirety of our relationship. Her heart is always searching for a way to help others, many times to the detriment of her own self. God certainly knew what he was doing to my benefit when He brought us together—her selflessness combined with my selfishness almost balances out to the benefit of the good. *Almost* simply because of the depth at which I operate can, unfortunately, overshadow the good she does. Like most things in my life, yet another area where I am constantly looking to improve, and she is always right beside me to encourage me and help me along that path.

After all these years, I still love to just talk to Trudi, to hold her hand, to open the door for her, and to honor her in every way I can. I always make sure the last words she hears from me are the same, whether on the phone as I leave for a trip, if she is off to teach her kindergarteners, or simply rolling over to call it a day. Those words are simple yet powerful: *I love you!* And that love has not wavered one bit in all our years together.

While this is a book about being a dad, I am convinced I could write a sequel about being a husband. Mind you, most of that book would probably be telling stories of how many mistakes I have made so far in this journey, and the beauty of forgiveness that my loving wife offers me, but we'll see about that topic later. In fact, as I wrote those words it inspired me to make some side notes and stop typing for a moment. I got up and went to find Trudi and told her that I had just had an epiphany and that my next book was going to be a joint effort—Trudi and me serving as co-authors on the process of developing as a husband! She remains a bit skeptical, but how fun will that be? So stay tuned. For now, it is important to me that I tell you a few more things about being a husband and how that evolves with time.

When we were young, everything was new, everything was spontaneous, and everything was about growing together and fun new adventures. As you grow together, kids enter the picture, and your focus ever so subtly shifts from each other to them. Enter the intentionality I mentioned earlier. It is easy to get totally lost in the lives of your kids and neglect each other. Combine that with careers and life in general, and it is easy to see how couples can drift apart. ***Make time for your wife.*** Time to honor and cherish her, time to talk to her, time to help her, time to simply sit and hold her hand. Plan and execute date nights on a consistent basis—it doesn't have to be big or expensive, just time for the two of you to be together. Do the dishes. Again, this an area of failure for me, but in most cases, whoever is reading this book, you know that she does the heavy lifting around the house: cooking, cleaning, taking care of the kids, and the list goes on. Be intentional to take some of this off of her plate. This is the voice of experience speaking, maybe not so much from my actual involvement, but from looking back and seeing the opportunities I have missed over the years to show her my love and appreciation. This will mean more to her than anything you could ever buy her or any place you could ever take her. I admit to abject failure in this area, but I am so thankful that Trudi is who she is and that she continued to deal with me and all of my shortcomings. I know how difficult I can be, but she is a special person in so many ways, more ways than I could ever detail in a book, but my love for her has never once waivered for even a second, and thankfully hers for me hasn't either.

You hear people talk about how couples grow apart during these years of development in their lives. I think this is real. You also hear about that empty nesting phase in life, and that is very real too! More to come on that in chapter thirteen, but just know there is a very bright light at the end of the tunnel, and no, it isn't a train but rather the sun shining bright and beckoning you toward a beach somewhere together.

You're beginning to get to know my wife in this book, and she remains the rock in my life to this very day. More beautiful than ever, a better mom than any, and my very best friend in life. The way she loves me and our kids, words simply cannot express what that means and the impact she has. From the time of our kids' conception, we prayed for their salvation. From that same time, we prayed for their future spouses. From that same time, Trudi never forgot to pray for me. She is a jewel in every capacity and a joy to all who know her, and she has made me the luckiest man alive for so many years now. As a husband, I'm still trying to improve, but I certainly wouldn't want to traverse this adventure with anyone else. As a husband, hear me on this: do not take your bride for granted. Of course, she will have faults and will sometimes fail. I caution you to love her through these rather than point them out to her. In your marriage and in life, picture a person who is better than you. Better in practicing patience, better in exuding confidence, better in problem-solving, better in sticky situations, just . . . *better*. Picture this person, then do all you can to be that person, or at a minimum the best version of yourself working toward that goal. As a husband, your wife deserves that from you. As *her* husband, Trudi deserves that from me. I will never stop in my attempts to get there.

Before I Was a Dad, I Was a Son-In-Law

It was a Wednesday evening in February of 1992. Trudi was at work in a local railroad museum (maybe the worst job ever), but I knew tonight was my night. I showed up unannounced at Trudi's house, and I asked her parents to sit with me. Trudi and I had been dating for nearly two years at this point, and it was time for the big question. I'm sure many think this tradition to be a bit old-fashioned, but before I could ask Trudi to marry me, I had to *and* wanted to get permission from her parents. Looking back, I probably should have garnered the approval from her brothers as well, but we love each other like real brothers to this day, so I guess that part worked out.

Her parents cried, and as you probably guessed by now, they said yes! A couple of weeks later, on Leap-Year Day, I took Trudi to the roof of the Peabody Hotel in Memphis, dropped to one knee, and asked her to marry me. Times were different then; there was no official photographer and no engagement party, and there were no social media posts—just an intimate moment between the two of us that we have never forgotten. Less than ten months later, I became a husband and a son-in-law, both of which have proven to be enormous blessings in my life.

BEFORE...

As with most things in life, being a son-in-law does not come with an instruction manual. Trudi's parents made it easy on me, and I acclimated quickly to what it was like to have a larger extended family that it was time to really get to know. Both Trudi and I come from such amazing and caring families, similar in many ways but also very different in others. I have a sister by birth, but suddenly I have two brothers by marriage. I have cousins by birth, but suddenly a whole group of people that I don't even know are now related to me by marriage. I have parents by birth, but now I have a new set of parents who love me because I love their daughter. That is a lot to take in but overwhelming in the very best way possible. Being a son-in-law has proven to be a spectacular ride for me, and the love I have for my new family is as strong as for my birth family. It goes full circle too, as Cam has married Glori, and we love her like our very own, welcoming in yet another set of extended family from her world. These connections are orchestrated by God, and if you embrace them, your world will open up in a brand new way. But don't just be a taker in this partnership. No, give into your new extended family, and your blessings will abound.

A case and point for those blessings. When my mom passed away, things shifted for me. My dad had already gone on to be with the Lord a few years prior, so with my mom's passing it was a whole new reality that my parents were really gone. I realize many people lose their parents as children or when they are young. Others, like me, have the blessing of growing up and starting our own lives before we lose those who raised us. While different, it is still a difficult time to process. I'll never forget a conversation I had with Trudi's mom not long after my mom went to be with the Lord. We were at our house and she hugged me and said that while she knew she was not my mom, she loved me and she would be here for me just like my mom had. She was willing to stand in that gap for me, and it strengthened our bond even further from that day forward. A few years later she went on to be with the Lord, passing peacefully in her sleep, but that time after my mom passed where Mrs. Thelma stood in the gap for me is something for which I will forever be grateful.

My bride was, and in some ways even to this day still is, a bit naive. I say that with the deepest love and affection for every single aspect of her, but it remains a bit funny to me just how sheltered she was. Trudi was in for a very long ride with me, one that included great bumps and curves, exciting and sudden shifts and turns, and ultimately a lifetime of just shaking her head at me and knowing that is just who I am. Through it all, her love for me still amazes me, still inspires me, and still gives me strength when I just can't find it on my own. God instilled these innate traits in her, and her parents developed them, brought them out in her, and taught her that it is nothing short of holy to love people with the depth that she does. I will forever be thankful to Mr. Charlie and Mrs. Thelma—they gave me the greatest gift possible, and to this day I hope and pray I honor them in how I love my wife.

Chapter 7

TAKE MY TIME

It is Saturday morning, any Saturday morning will do, and McDonald's is calling our names. That may not sound exciting or even appetizing to most, but for me, these Saturdays are some of my best memories as a dad. Most likely it is around 8:30 a.m., but when we make our exit from the house, there is no clock on us, no real plan, and no telling what we might bring back home. We know there will be food, a toy store, maybe a playground, and lots of laughs, and that is enough for me. What is this time I'm going on about? Why of course, it's *Daddy Time*, and this is a time I wouldn't trade for anything in the world. We even had our own song about Daddy Time, plagiarizing on the introductory tune from *Veggie Tales* but making up our own words to make it our very own!

It was a rite of passage with each of our kids. Every single Saturday morning we would head out for Daddy time. With Lauren, it started a little earlier than with Cam and Emma, but when it was just us, there really weren't many rules. Once each child reached the age of two years old, their adventures with Daddy time began. Until then, they stayed at home anxiously awaiting our return to hear all about our great adventures of the morning. I could be exaggerating about their anticipation of said return, but hey, why not? As I mentioned, the day typically started at McDonald's or Dunkin Donuts—where we landed was completely arbitrary. But the time together was anything but! We talked about anything and everything. I'm sure as they got a little older I embarrassed them more than once, but I treasured this time with my kids and held onto it like it was more precious than gold.

Most things I do in life require a fairly detailed agenda, I just can't seem to relax without a plan, but these times were purposefully unstructured so that each child could take creative license on what that time looked like. Being the oldest, Lauren took charge most days, even when it was all four of us, but then again, she had the most experience with this wonderful adventure we held so close. As I mentioned, there was always food, always some form of entertainment, and almost always a prize to take home and show off to Trudi. We didn't spend much money, but the time we spent together remains simply priceless to me.

Here is my *first* recommendation to you: **make your own version of Daddy Time** a priority in the life of you and your kids. You will never regret a single minute of it. And by the way, your wife will thank you too. I wish I could say that Trudi spent every one of those Saturday mornings sitting by the pool or shopping or hanging out with friends, but that wouldn't be true. In fact, the quiet time was a welcome change for her. She was a stay-at-home mom for about eleven years, and a small break from the demands of the kids was a welcome addition to her schedule as well. She did a lot of house cleaning during that time, but in my mind, I just like to picture her relaxing and enjoying the peace and quiet that she so richly deserved.

But beware, Daddy Time, like most great things in life, will be fleeting. As the kids grow, their interests diverge, and your Saturdays will be taken from you. Not that it is a bad thing—your time simply shifts in a new direction with other activities like sports and such—but that alone time, that specifically regarded and highly anticipated time alone with just Dad and the kids, it will evolve, and before you know it, it has slipped by. It is the nature of how they grow up, but while you have the opportunity, I recommend you do everything in your power to hold on tight, make it fun, create those memories, and show your kids just how much you love spending time with them. It will come back to you a hundredfold, and you will forever remember Daddy Time as some of the best times ever. I can't say my kids took great strides intellectually, academically, athletically, or in any other way as a result of Daddy Time, but they sure loved spending that time with dear old Dad, and as that dear old Dad, I would give anything to be able to go back and do it all over again.

Now more on the value of spending time with your crew. Vacations are a must, and we have taken lots of them. My favorite places are Destin, FL, and Disney World (the one in Orlando). For many years I am sure that our kids thought those were the only two places where people went for vacation. There have been trips to the mountains, to the Midwest, and to a couple of other outliers, but through the years we became regulars at the two aforementioned vacation spots. And I loved every single minute of it. Trudi, maybe not so much. She wants to go out West, to New York, just anywhere different. Now that our lives are turning into the empty nester phase, those trips are underway, and more are on the horizon.

Each of our kids had their first visit to Disney by the time they were three years old. At that time, they were actually free until they turned three, so there was a bit of a method to our madness on that one. It is hard to count how many times we have made that journey, but it pales in comparison to the number of times we have gone to the beach. That could very well be part of the reason that Lauren decided to move to the beach, so I have re-thought those trips if indeed that played into it. But as long as she is following God's will for her life, I will not get in the way! This brings me to my *second* bit of advice: **take the time to get away**. It doesn't matter what your financial situation looks like; find a way.

It was the summer of 2016, and we had Lauren's senior trip planned for the summer after her graduation from high school. We were headed down to 30A, a little higher-end version of what we affectionately call the Redneck Riviera, and our condo awaited. The thing is, about three weeks before we were to head down to the coast, I lost my job. But we never really hesitated to continue on our path to the beach. Sounds pretty dumb, right? Go ahead and go to the beach even without a job! But it was not a mistake as it served as a galvanizing time for our family when so many things around us were chaotic. Admittedly there were a couple of times during that trip when I was mentally preoccupied, wondering where the fate of my career might lead, but as always, Trudi was right there to pray with me and for me, to reassure me, and to encourage me to relax and enjoy the ride.

Of course, the gentle lapping of those waves as they came ashore did indeed serve to calm my nerves, and we had an incredible trip together. Yes, the Lord had a plan as He always does, and I moved right on into the next phase of my career not long after our return home. Looking back, it is my hope that the kids learned a little bit about faith from that trip—that it is OK to forge ahead when the future seems a bit unclear, and that indeed, family does matter and the time together always proves invaluable.

You do not have to spend a lot of money to take a vacation. Get creative, do your research, and find times for long weekends where you simply get out of your normal routine—whatever you can do to spend quality time away from your normal lives so that you can be together and grow together. Again, these are times you will never regret, and I assure you that the window to pull this off will slip away before you know it, and your kids will be otherwise engaged and not available. Remind yourself to take *my* time, and give it freely to those you love most.

Then there is their *stuff*. Growing up, my parents were not readily available to attend most of my events. Whether it was a sporting event, a singing event, or something in the theater, they missed a lot. I never thought much of it, as it was just normal for us. But when Trudi and I had our own kids, I knew how important it was that I be there. I am so thankful that over the years I was blessed with enough flexibility that I hardly ever missed a practice, much less an actual event for any of my kids. And once again, that time afforded with them and those experiences are simply irreplaceable. I'm sure any one of our kids would have preferred we not always be *so* present, particularly at their practices, but those are precious times, and I look forward to more of the same when grandkids become part of our equation.

TAKE MY TIME

Third piece of advice: **make it a priority to be at their *stuff*.** No matter what it is, even if you don't understand it or don't even like it very much, be there! I always told our kids to be passionate about *something*. It doesn't matter if that something is sports, theater, cheer, music, art, or anything else—just find your passion and pursue it with everything you have. Life is just better when you are deep within your passion; be sure your kids know this and find this.

Trudi and I decided early on that our kids would not sleep in the bed with us. I am not here to judge if that is what you choose or not—that is a very personal and private decision that you have to make. For us, it was an easy one. That said, there was a compromise that we lived with for many years to come. At any given time, we might have one, two, or three kids sleeping on the floor in our bedroom. We even had these pallets rolled up and stored under our bed so they were not just on the floor—I mean, we are not animals, right? Each night they would start their sleep in their own beds, but inevitably they would migrate to our room, pull out said pallets, and sleep right there on the floor in our room with us. Remember how I said I wouldn't judge? I ask the same from you! It seemed to bring our kids peace to be in the room with us, and truth be told, we liked having them so close to us as well.

As they grew, this practice evolved a bit. Once they found it more practical to sleep in their own beds, we thought we had entered a new phase of parenting. And we were right, just not exactly in the way we thought. They were now determined to sleep in their own beds, but not without a little bit of overwatch from one of us in the hallway outside their rooms. I can't count the nights I sat outside their rooms, in different houses as we moved to a couple of new locations as they grew as well. From time to time I would try to sneak away but would invariably get caught by one of them who had not yet dozed off. This went on for quite some time, in fact the first time I read the Bible in its entirety, every word was consumed sitting in the hallway outside of their rooms! That turned out to be time very well spent, albeit maybe a bit odd in the way it transpired. Again, no matter what little anomalies or idiosyncrasies you develop with your kids' bedtime routine, make it count. Kneeling beside each of their beds each night, praying with them and for them, is yet another memory that I will forever cherish. *Fourth, fifth,* and *sixth* bit of advice: take the time to **pray with your kids,** to **love on them at bedtime,** and to **be patient with them** as they figure out what makes them feel safe and loved each night.

As I write this morning, I am sitting on the balcony of my hotel in Florida. It is another one of those Saturday mornings I opened this chapter with, only this time Trudi and I have traveled down to visit with Lauren. It is early, it is raining, and the only sounds I hear are seagulls mewing and the soft crashing of waves into the sand. As I look out across the horizon, I am nearly overwhelmed by the beauty of God's creation. I love the beach. A melanoma diagnosis has changed my approach to it for sure, but I still love it, and if you asked me where my "place" is, there is no doubt it is right here. Once again I am alluding to taking *my* time. And my bit of advice for you at this spot: **take *your* time.** Take your time to stop and smell the roses. Take your time to drive seven hours just to spend a couple of days with your baby girl. Take your time to gaze across the horizon and contemplate God's vastness and creation. Take your time for your family.

We'll have brunch with Lauren, hang out with her and her roommates for a bit, laugh and talk about the present, the past, the future. And in a couple of days when we head home, the time will have passed all too quickly. You see, we are so very proud of Lauren for taking this leap. For going out on her own and living a life worth telling stories about. For doing what most people never do—take a leap of faith. But when we depart, it will be as though it is for the first time when she left home. The heartache is real, the emptiness in our hearts is real, and yes, the tears are real. You see, no matter how proud we may be, no matter what path our kids take, no matter how close or how far away, *my* kids will forever occupy a huge, special place in my heart. I want to hug them and hold them close and be able to go upstairs and check on them while they sleep. That is not the reality we face, but we can take *our* time and go to them, be available to them, pray for them, and forever love them.

I would love to say that I have been completely present and available at all times to our kids and to Trudi. But I committed to being honest and transparent with you when I decided to write this book, so this is one of those peek-behind-the-curtain moments. While I may have been present at every event, at home after work, and even at bedtime, being present is sometimes all I really was—I was just there. I may have been there physically, but far too often I was not fully engaged and fully attentive. I can't count how many evenings we were together as a family, but there I was with my laptop, playing catch-up on emails, evaluating projects, or developing new business plans. I honed incredibly selective hearing, and my entire family will attest to that fact to this day. This waste of my actual presence is something I can never get back, and something I regret fully.

I include this disclaimer simply because I want to be real with you. In today's world of "everybody's life is great" on social media, I think we all need a dose of reality. I wish I had been a better dad, a better husband, a better person for the entirety of my life, but I am a flawed human—made in God's image, but a failed version to put it mildly. To me, it really isn't about how great you or I can be, but rather the never-ending pursuit of that accolade from our loved ones where they know we gave it our all, and even when we failed, we always meant well. It has been said that perfect is the enemy of good. Outside of Jesus, none of us are perfect. But even the *pursuit* of perfect can be to the detriment of the good. If my wife and my kids know I love them with my full heart, then perfect, good, or even average are all simple titles for the effort we put forth. My *final* bit of advice for you in this chapter: **be fully present**, **love them with everything you have**, and **put the laptop away**—your job or employer must not rob you of those precious moments that you have with your family. Your company will replace you in a heartbeat, but your family—*your* family—seek and find your identity right there, and always remember to *take my time!*

Chapter 8

PETS, FRIENDS, AND SPORTS

From time to time around our house, as our kids were growing up, I would offer the following advice: "Don't do anything that starts with, *Hey, watch this!*" That is a variation on the all-time great parenting scenario of, *If your friends all jumped off a bridge, does that mean you should too?*—but maybe just a bit more of a proactive variation. We always encouraged our kids to be adventurous within reason. Life is more fun with a little adventure, and again, it just makes for better stories!

Parents throughout time have had different takes on the best approach to raising their kids—that is no secret. I am not a big believer in templates for anything. What I mean by that is simple: what works for one person, opportunity, scenario, or whatever, just might not be the right thing for another. That is probably most true in parenting, as the variables that impact us are infinite. That said, there is another bit of advice I will drop for you right here: **talk to your kids**. Open, transparent, honest communication will save you and your kids a vast amount of heartache, and it might just keep them on the right path from time to time as well. Is that a simple word of advice? Of course! I've never claimed to be the smartest guy in the room; we are all in trouble if indeed that is ever the case. But even I know that the ability to relate, the ability to influence, the ability to succeed, the ability to connect all come from open lines of communication.

Is this easy? I think you already know the answer to that one. Who among us really wants to sit down and talk to our kids about all of those uncomfortable things in life, like sex, drinking, and drugs? Maybe there are unicorns out there that covet that time and look forward to the day when these conversations are important, but that does not apply to the masses. Of course, Trudi and I took on the responsibility of these basic conversations at the appropriate time in the lives and growth of our kids—it would have been irresponsible not to. But more important than those early conversations was the open pipeline that we encouraged throughout the development of our children's lives. As you know, it is different for boys and for girls. Middle school is a beast for both, to say the least! But by always encouraging our kids to talk to us about what they are experiencing on a day-in and day-out basis, I am confident that we avoided many of the pitfalls that so many children and teens fall into. Thinking back, there actually were not that many times when we engaged in a difficult conversation about what our kids were facing in each of their lives, but I am equally confident that there was never a doubt in any of their minds that no topic was off limits, no subject was too difficult to broach, and ultimately we could talk through whatever was happening in their lives and together—keyword, *together*—find a solution, or at worst find a way to weather the storm.

That said, I'm taking on three big areas in this particular chapter: *sports, friends,* and *pets.* While all of these do not necessarily revolve around difficult conversations, open communication remains a must. Let's start at the end and work our way back....

Pets

I grew up with all kinds of pets. At any given time, we would have three or four dogs, so it goes without saying that I love them as pets.

PETS, FRIENDS, AND SPORTS

Trudi on the other hand, not so much. Earlier I introduced you to Skippy, our Pekinese, but there is more to the story of that little handful. The pets in the Presley household have been fairly few if not far between. Outside of Skippy, our first pet with the kids was Bubbles, the Beta fish. If you know anything about fish, you already know they are simply boring as pets. Bubbles was a pretty fish and graceful around his bowl, but that bowl got nasty really quick, and it would smell bad just as quickly. There were a few times we thought we had lost Bubbles before his time actually came, but he fought through. There was the time we went on vacation and forgot to set up someone to feed him. Bad parenting, bad pet owners, but he survived and came back to thrive. There was the time our friend's young son stopped by and proceeded to try and spear Bubbles with a pencil, but once again he survived, going on to live a nice long fish life. The death of Bubbles was less traumatic than we might have imagined, but of course, we held the dedicated flushing funeral to honor his passing.

Next enters Boots, our dwarf bunny. Boots was aptly named as he was solid black except for the white caps on his feet, thus the appropriate moniker. Where Bubbles was primarily Lauren's pet, Boots was Cam's. The whole family loved Boots—who doesn't love a cute, cuddly little bunny. Cam *really* loved that rabbit though. He would cuddle with him when he took naps, and it was the cutest thing ever. Not an option with Bubbles as you can imagine! Boots would chew on the wrapping paper on Christmas presents and run full speed around our living area, adding lots of laughs to our family. As it was with Bubbles, it was supposed to be the kids' responsibility to clean their pet's living area, whether it was a bowl or a cage. If you are a parent with pets, you can already guess who did the majority of those cleanings. If you have not yet had this experience, just hear me on this. Your kids will promise you anything and everything in order to sway you toward their position on a pet. Oh, the promises that will be made to you! But beware, while their intentions are pure of heart, their actions will fall miserably short when it comes to their follow-through. Write it down and memorize it because that is exactly how it will go down. Case in point: that rabbit cage would get, well, cagey, and it was quite a job to clean it and restock it, most of the time done by yours truly. Even so, Boots was a great pet, and one night he simply passed in his sleep. Cam was devastated at the loss of his little friend, showing such a kind heart as he missed his favorite pet. We "buried" Boots in a shoe box, wrapped in duct tape, and set it free down a small creek not far from our house. I'm not sure if that was the right farewell, or even if it was legal, but it served the moment well.

Somewhere along our path, we decided we needed a cat. This is a definite deviation from how we do things at the Presley household, as not a single one of us would consider ourselves a "cat person." That said, it only took a snake in the garage to slither across Trudi's feet one morning to solidify the need to bring in a pet we would have not considered otherwise. Enter Elvis to the fold. Elvis was a freebie that we procured from a friend of a friend, and admittedly he was a cute little guy. He lived outside, sleeping in our garage (remember the catalyst that drove us to this decision in the first place).

Elvis grew up, and he was fine, but then one day he was just gone. Never saw him again, never heard from him again, never received even a postcard from him! Just gone! I guess that can be the nature of cats, here today and gone tomorrow. But then there was Carl. Carl the cat wandered into our lives one day and sort of adopted us. Actually, Lauren is a bit of a cat whisperer, so when Carl came around, she drew him in. We tried to think of the most asinine name we could for a cat, thus *Carl*, but Carl proved to be a bit aloof at a minimum. He would come and go, but he seemed to always be around. He was a good-looking cat and served the same purpose as Elvis, keeping the snakes at bay. Carl would climb up our garage entry door to the house, hang onto the doorknob, and peer into the house, checking on us to see what we were up to. It was an odd activity, at least to us, but he seemed content hanging out there and just watching through the window.

I mentioned that Carl would wander in and out of our lives for some time, always returning after a day or two. Once he came home and had a new injury, a rip in his right ear, proving he was out getting into trouble in places unbeknownst to us. Carl the cat now had a very distinguishing scar, further setting him apart from the herd. Then one day he left, and we didn't hear from him for months. We assumed he had gone out and picked a fight he couldn't win.

On a random Saturday, out of the blue, Cam and I were out in the driveway shooting basketball, and Carl appeared once again. Again, he looked a little worse for wear, but there he was. We welcomed him back, and he hung around for a while again, picking right back up by climbing the door and peeking in the house. Then, like Elvis, he was gone. We never heard from Carl again, but we hope he landed at another house with another family who would feed him and allow him to climb up their door and watch them live their lives through the looking glass.

Our current pet has been with us for over eight years at the time of this writing. "Ace" is our eighty-pound purebred black Labrador retriever, and he is a good boy. Emma was terrified of him as his growth certainly outpaced hers, but Ace has helped her transform from a little girl scared of dogs into a young woman working as a pet sitter (among other jobs—the regular entrepreneur!) during her summers home from college. There has never been a cuter puppy than Ace. Ace was easy to pick from his litter. Cam has a white spot in his hair that has always been a unique aspect for him, and when we saw this solid black puppy with a white spot, we knew he was the one. If you know anything about labs, they chew every single thing they encounter as puppies. Ace was no exception, and we wondered if indeed we had chosen wisely. But over time he outgrew that habit and settled into simply being part of our family. He oversees his domain (our backyard) with pride and only utilizes his *mean bark* if someone happens to enter his domain unannounced. He is a protector of our family without a doubt and a big baby to boot! He loves attention, particularly from the kids, even the neighborhood kids, but is content to keep watch over the yard, swim near constantly in our pool, and sleep about twenty hours a day. They say it is a dog's life for a reason, and I'd say Ace lives that life well!

Friends

As our kids grew up, we found, like most people, that whatever sport or activity they were involved in created not only their circle of friends but the same for my wife and I as well. Through dance, all kinds of sports, cheer, church, and whatever else occupied their time, we found ourselves drawn to their side along with the parents of the other kids involved in similar activities. But here is the caveat I want to unpack with you: our kids never really ran in the *popular* crowd, and I am convinced that was to their advantage.

Lauren, Cam, and Emma are all very smart in different ways, very talented in different ways, as well as entertained in different ways. Each of them adopted a very strong aversion to simply following the crowd—that is where I think it served them well to not necessarily always run with the "in" crowd. When kids are young, they don't have much say in where they go, what they do, or who they hang out with. At least that was the way it was in our house. Enter middle school. It is in this pivotal and unusually difficult time that the separation begins. This is the point where you begin to experience just how difficult it can be to see your child left out. No matter how hard they may try, or *we* may try, kids will indeed be cruel, and it was no different for mine as they were the recipients of their fair share of targeted stupidity.

Through those tough middle school years, I found it to be somewhat easier on Cam than on either Lauren or Emma. There are six years between Lauren and Emma, so even though a lot can change in that time, we found that the mean girl syndrome was still very much in existence. My girls fell victim to this just like so many others through the years. It was different for Cam as he was the quarterback on the football team, the point guard on the basketball team, and the shortstop on the baseball team—all positions of leadership and acceptance—so it made his middle school life different, if not easier than the girls. Is that fair? Absolutely not! But if you have not yet experienced this with your own kids, you will, and it is a heart-wrenching time as a parent. What we found, however, was that it was a time of growth for all three of them, and we had to let them find their way through the obstacles that middle school presented. They survived, maybe even thrived at times, and guess what? Your kids will too.

High School was another interesting time of development in the lives of our kids. While Lauren and Cam crossed over each other with their age difference being only two school years apart, Emma came in the year after Cam graduated, thus following in the footsteps of both Lauren and Cam. I'll go ahead and let you in on a little secret: she nailed it and thrived in their footsteps, blazing her own path and navigating the perils she faced with grace and dignity. That said, the idea of wanting to be part of the "in" crowd didn't chase my kids here either. They were perfectly fine with being true to themselves and owning their own path. I'm sure there were times they would have preferred to be included in things they missed, but they had their people, and as I already stated, I am convinced that this was to their advantage in the long run. We all make mistakes, but if your kids run in the wrong crowds, the chances are exponentially higher that those mistakes will be compounded and will follow them as they continue to grow and mature.

Both of the girls did just fine, being voted onto their respective homecoming courts and for the most part, just being friendly with almost everyone rather than just that coveted popular group. Neither of our girls really dated anyone seriously in high school, another big advantage to them (and to dear old Dad!) in my opinion. They both chose to keep their friend group pretty tight, though, and found themselves most of the time with only one or two really close friends. It has been said that if you have one true friend in life then you should consider yourself blessed. I agree that it is indeed a blessing to have one good friend, but in high school that can become a limiting factor because, let's face it, it's high school, and there is a lot of drama with that.

I saw Lauren and Emma at times on the outside looking in, and as their dad, it not only hurt me, but at times it made me angry! Teenage girls can be very cruel, and the world of social media has made that even worse. Now, everybody knows exactly what everyone else is doing because every move is posted, tweeted, or found on BeReal. If that doesn't take place, they all track each other's every move on Snapchat so the proverbial "fomo" is very real. With girls today, for almost any age now, it seems that every event, every happening, every turn of the corner simply exists for the right photo op so it can be posted. I really can't understand the pressure that young girls must feel today by this phenomenon, constantly driven to post the perfect picture to portray the perfect life, when all the while inwardly feeling inadequate or just trying to fit in or keep up. That pressure is unrelenting, so dads, hear me on this: it is more important than ever that you reassure your kids, and your *girls* in particular, of their worth, their worthiness, and your undying love for them. They must know that in a world of superficial praise and falsely inflated lifestyles, your love for them remains unwavering and genuine. No matter what else they face, they need this cornerstone in their lives, and only you can provide that for them. Step up and own this; you will never regret it.

There is a phenomenon called allodoxaphobia, and simply stated, that is the fear of what others' opinions of you might be. Cam certainly never suffered from this erroneous thought process. He was always secure in who he was and fine with going it alone if necessary. I already mentioned he played all the major sports through middle school and even into his freshman year. As he began to lose interest in some of them, our standing rule of "if you start a season, you finish the season" was enacted, which ultimately sparked his tennis career. We found that just as when he was younger, those he played with were those he stayed with. He had friends but maybe not a best friend. He was perfectly fine to stay at home or go to the courts and work on his game all by himself. While Trudi and I often worried about Cam as well as the girls when they seemed to be alone, it never really appeared to surface with them. In the end, it is my opinion that they grew stronger as a result of this, became a bit more self-sufficient, and ultimately, learned that they are strong, smart, and capable, all of which will serve them well for their entire lives.

Sports

Without a doubt, sports played a big part in the lives of our family as our kids grew up. Let me be clear, no parent should ever make their child think their worth or their love is contingent on success in any activity, much less in sports, but the lessons that can be learned through organized competition do prove to be invaluable. Let's take a look at their involvement in sports one by one.

Lauren

It is safe to say that by most standards Lauren would not be considered an outstanding athlete. As we have already discussed, she was the girliest of girls growing up and did not participate in any organized sports until she was in fifth grade. Enter tennis into her world.

I've been involved in playing, teaching, or coaching tennis since I was fourteen years old. While that does not guarantee expertise, or in some cases even proficiency, it does give me many years of perspective and experience in and around the game. Tennis was a great fit for Lauren and would prove to be a big part of her life development.

Lauren was a typical fifth-grade girl. A bit gangly, she was tall and admittedly unathletic on the court, but she wanted to learn. Early on she took private lessons from a local legend in the field of tennis instruction: James Parker. To this day I can still hear and see James teaching Lauren the three-ball drill for the development of her backhand and him trying to teach her the nuances of the toss for her serve. That latter part was indeed a challenge, but that backhand . . . well that was a different story.

Over time, Lauren developed what I still consider to be the best high school girl's backhand in the area during her time. Lauren would still not have been described as an athlete, but with work and dedication, I saw her develop into an accomplished tennis player. Early in her high school career, she would move on from James to another popular local tennis pro, Ted Measley. Ted helped her develop her overall skillset further, infusing both skill and strategy into her game, and she went on to an incredibly successful tennis career, culminating with a state runner-up finish in her senior year. Tennis was good for Lauren, and I still remember her final point at the state tournament. I walked out on the court and hugged her as she and I both cried, not so much because she lost but probably more because I was so incredibly proud of her and that an important phase in her life had come to an end. I'm reminded of the famous quote from Dr. Seuss that says, "Don't cry because it's over, smile because it happened." That is great advice to take away from this stage in life.

Tennis taught Lauren to believe in herself and to stand up for herself. The sport helped transform a quiet, somewhat introverted little girl into a confident young woman who was a force to be reckoned with. I remember with great pride the attitude she played with on the court and the way she would stand up to those who would attempt to cheat her on that same court. They learned quickly that such indiscretions would not be tolerated and that she would call them out in a heartbeat. That lesson along with the general life lessons of the rewards of hard work are carried with her to this very day, and I must add, fill this old dad's heart with pride! Tennis was good for Lauren, and I wouldn't trade a single minute of watching her on the court for anything.

Cam

I'll be brutally honest here, Cam was a fat baby. Even at his earliest doctor appointments, he would weigh in above the ninety-fifth percentile, and the doctors projected him to be six feet two and two hundred twenty pounds by the time he was in high school. As his dad, I figured I had a lineman on my hands! As time went by, Cam did indeed hit that six feet two height, but the two hundred twenty never developed. At his heaviest, he probably hit 175, but boy what an athlete he was becoming.

Baseball was his early sport, starting T-ball at the young age of four. He loved this, and we loved this, although as time went by I'm not so sure his sisters always enjoyed the weekends spent at the ballpark. Cam settled in very quickly as the shortstop on any team he was a part of. He played little league and at the age of nine transitioned into the world of travel ball. I decided to start a new team from scratch, so along with a couple of buddies of mine who had boys the same age as Cam, we launched the Vipers. What a strong name, right? Menacing, intimidating, dangerous to some, but feared by all. Well, that is all fine and good, but at first, we were none of those things! To say the least, the Vipers were not great their first year, winning only one game, but in the five years that the team existed, we became a force to be reckoned with, and we had a blast. Those red and black uniforms still hang in my closet along with some of the ball caps that we redesigned each year. Our best year we finished first in our state, although we lost in the championship game. But we still had enough points to claim the prize. The lessons learned from travel ball are enough to fill a separate book, so maybe look for that one day.

Cam's introduction to basketball came through a Christian league called Upward. I coached this team too, and it was quite funny to watch a bunch of four- and five-year-olds attempt anything productive on the court. Lauren was a part of the cheerleading squad for the Upward teams, so once again we were usually somewhere in a gym or a field most weekends revolving around sports.

Cam went on to play basketball through his freshman year of high school, including a travel team for this as well. He moved from the point position and mainly played the two or three spots on the court as he was getting taller than most of his teammates. His defensive intensity cost him two broken noses during his basketball days, but I absolutely loved to watch him play defense. This tenacity would prove itself to be an asset to him in all aspects of his life as he grew up.

Football was a different story. Cam played fifth- and sixth-grade football for his school, where once again I was his coach. Cam had an incredible arm, proven as a shortstop in baseball, so he settled in as quarterback for most of his early football run. He continued to work very hard and prove he not only had talent but the drive to succeed in any sport. Middle school football proved to be the time when once again his defensive prowess would shine through. He continued to play either quarterback or wide receiver on offense, but as a defensive back, he had a great read of the field. His catch across the middle for a forty-yard touchdown against his biggest rival school, along with his sixty-five-yard pick-six against the other hometown rival remain my two favorite memories of Cam on the football field.

And then there was the time when he met Trey Smith on the field. Trey is a starting offensive tackle for the Super Bowl Champions Kansas City Chiefs as I pen this book, but Cam met him when he was a seventh grader and Trey was an eighth grader. Trey played for the aforementioned cross-town rival, and as an eighth grader, he seemed to already be the same size he is today, destined for his pro career. We ran an offense that gave Cam the ability to decide whether to run or pass, and this time he made the wrong choice. He faked the pitch out to his running back but tucked the ball back in and turned up-field. Trey was on defense, in fact, he basically was their defense, and Cam ran straight into him. I would love to say that Cam juked him out and ran around the edge to score the winning touchdown. But that's not what happened. No, Trey grabbed him and basically drove Cam straight into the dirt! We were not sure if he would ever get up again, but true to Cam's form, he managed to find his feet and stayed in the game. Needless to say, he opted to get rid of the ball quickly for the rest of that game—lesson learned.

As good as Cam was in his early sports, it was a trip to the state championships by Lauren in tennis that would set his athletic course throughout high school. We went to Murfreesboro, TN, for these competitions each year as Lauren and her high school team would qualify year after year. Cam saw this at the end of his eighth-grade year and decided that was his athletic calling. From there he put in countless hours on the court—lessons, clinics, solo hitting on our ball machine, serving hundreds of balls a day, and then traveling around the southeast for tournament play. Cam would go on to win a TSSAA individual state championship as well as a team state championship, and I must say the time he spent on the court could also produce another book. Maybe the athletic side of being a dad is a whole new undertaking worth writing about? Time will tell.

Running is another part of Cam's life that can't be overlooked. I have been a runner for over thirty years now, starting after college graduation, and I simply love it. Cam never really got the running bug early in his life, but after college, he too began to take it seriously. In fact, late in 2023, he ran the full St. Jude Marathon in Memphis, while his wife, Glori, ran the half marathon the same day. What an accomplishment for both of them, and as always I am very proud. In May of 2024, Cam organized and ran a solo ultramarathon, a fifty miler where he was the sole participant, all to raise money for Young Life kids to be able to go to camp. I say he was a solo runner, but he did have pacers alongside him for four out of the five, ten-mile legs of the race. It was my honor, and an incredibly special time for me, as I was able to be his pacer for one of the ten-mile legs of the race. This was an incredible time together for us, and even though it was pouring rain for the entire leg, we laughed and talked the whole time. I would not trade a single minute of that time with him as he took on this noble effort for a great cause. Still more proof that sports can and do play a role in the character development of our kids and yours as well.

Emma

Let me be clear: I hate Atlanta. No offense to you if that is your home, but it simply is not for me. I sometimes work in Atlanta, but Emma's cheer team competed multiple times in the largest competition of its kind in the world there, and when there are twenty-two thousand cheerleaders, not to mention the high-maintenance moms and cheer dads, it is a lot. More on that in a moment.

It was February of 2021, and we were in Atlanta for a competition. The last time we were here, Emma's team won the event, and that in and of itself softened the blow of all things Atlanta. Not the case for this trip, so after considerable delays in wrapping things up, we head home. Normally a six-hour drive for us, this one would prove to be much different. We knew bad weather was a possibility, so we got on the road as quickly as possible, but we were not fast enough, unfortunately. About halfway into our drive, the snow started falling. It was already below freezing, so the impact on the roads was practically immediate. This was the kind of snow that our friends in Minnesota are completely accustomed to, but we southern dwellers are simply not equipped for this. The snow was coming down in sheets, and the driving conditions deteriorated so fast that we couldn't adapt our route in time to avoid it. Suffice it to say that what would normally be a six-hour drive turned into a nine-hour drive, and it did nothing but solidify my opening statement about Atlanta. Atlanta might simply be where I lay the blame for that situation as it certainly is not at fault, but it was closely associated so therefore it gets blamed. Perfectly logical, right? Well, on with Emma's story.

Those who know me have often heard me say that if three kids can be opposites, then that is exactly what mine are: opposites. That said, at least in the sports realm, they had one area of common ground—tennis. For Emma, it was somewhat of an afterthought, and I'll always believe she played the sport just for me. That was never a reason or rationale that I pushed on our kids, simply to do something to appease us, but either way, she jumped in. And the results were amazing! If she had chosen to really pursue it, she would have easily been the number one player on our high school team and had opportunities to play in college. But that simply was not her passion, so after two seasons, she decided to step away for her senior year and focus on where her true passion really existed and thrived: cheer.

Much like Lauren, sports did not dictate so many moves in Emma's life early on. As I mentioned, much of her time was spent being dragged around to Cam's ball games and matches. But around age nine, we entered an arena I never thought I would have any part of—the world of all-star competitive cheer. And boy oh boy, I had no idea what I was in for!

Let me be clear, at first I didn't fully respect the athleticism and discipline required to excel in this sport, and yes, I do classify this as a sport. At least now I do! Cheer might have proven to be the most expensive sport that any of our kids participated in, but just like every dime we invested into Lauren and Cam's sports ventures, everything we did for Emma was just as worth it. If you have not lived the life of a cheer dad, well let me say, it is quite different from other sports. Some will tell you that the moms are a problem in competitive cheer. That their high-maintenance histrionics can make the experience unbearable. In some cases that might be true, but since this is a book directed primarily toward dads, let me expound a bit on that front.

Admittedly I saw some dads who took it too far in my opinion, all decked out in lavish costumes, sometimes including flashing lights and platform shoes, but I quickly determined those outfits said more about that dad in particular than anything to do with his cheerleader or her team. Suffice it to say, if you enter the world of competitive cheer, buckle in as it will be a whirlwind of a ride, and your wallet will feel it.

Emma was blessed to be a part of a wonderful gym named Jackson Cheer, owned by a husband and wife team. Robert and Hollie Farmer poured into these athletes, and in Emma's case, she grew immensely from them and the experiences they provided. I'll never forget watching them pray together as a team to conclude practices, even if things had not gone swimmingly during their time on the mat. Hollie treated her teams like they were her own kids, getting on to them when she didn't see the effort she wanted and loving on them no matter what. Every kid needs a coach or some outside influence other than Mom and Dad to show them love, discipline, and support, and for all that Robert and Hollie gave Emma, I will forever be grateful.

Cheer did another thing for Emma and our family—it afforded us the opportunity to travel all around the southeastern part of the United States to compete. From huge competitions in Atlanta, Orlando, Chattanooga, and Sevierville, to tiny towns where the cheer competition doubled the population of said location for that weekend. These were some long days; however, in all-star cheer, their routine is two-and-a-half minutes in length. That's it, just two-and-a-half minutes. They go hard for that time, and it is amazing to watch, but it is still less than three minutes to compete. Then, you wait. You wait through all the other teams competing, you wait through the dance party that inevitably breaks out before awards, you wait through awards. And that is just a single-day event. Some are two-day events, so you get double the everything, including the downtime. You have driven sometimes four, six, eight, or thirteen hours to get there, and they go hard for two-and-a-half minutes, and you wait. But let me tell you, that downtime is where we developed some of our most cherished friendships to this day.

Don't discount the downtime; that can be where the magic happens. I can confidently say I do not regret a single minute or dollar invested in Emma's time as a competitive cheerleader. In fact, I applaud her for taking that leap, and I thank her for helping me expand my horizons and learn a new level of respect for her and her chosen field of expertise.

All Three

As I wrap up this segment on the impact of sports on the lives of our kids and our family as a whole, I will tell you with all confidence, sports enhanced and enriched our lives as Lauren, Cam, and Emma grew up. That is a massive understatement but a concise summary.

The lessons that each of them learned and still carry with them today—confidence, boldness, teamwork, the thrill of victory, and the agony of defeat—all of these are character builders, and character conquers much difficulty that we all face.

In the sports I have had the privilege to coach, I put an emphasis on "touch the line." There are many conditioning drills that involve a back-and-forth run, applying, preparing, and benefiting each athlete in many ways. But as you turn, the expectation is that you touch the line. Most will simply turn and not make the extra effort to bend down and touch the line. There is no real cardiovascular advantage to touching the line; rather, it is the discipline involved. Sports, just like life, require discipline. Discipline conquers all when motivation and inspiration fade. I watched my kids soar to the highest heights in their competitive undertakings, and I also watched them through their lowest lows. But the discipline it took to even compete—that is the takeaway that best serves them to this day.

I love the time I spent watching and coaching our kids over the years. It is something I will forever cherish, and I will tell story after story about these escapades as long as I have breath in my body. It brings me joy to think back, to reminisce, and when I really contemplate these times, it usually brings both tears and joy. No matter if your kids are athletes or not, it really doesn't matter. Just be sure and instill in them that they must find their passion and pour themselves into it. The experiences, the friends, the impact on their lives, and quite frankly on ours, will prove simply to be immeasurable, and the memories of the good and bad times will give you comfort and joy as you relive moments well down the road in your own life.

Chapter 9

DADS

This book is built on the stories of three dads: *mine, Trudi's,* and then there is *Me*. All three men are very different but also share some common characteristics. I am a product of their influence as a dad, and I can only hope that my kids will take the lessons learned through both my influence and my mistakes and prepare them for their future as a husband, as wives, and as parents.

My Dad

Thinking through what it was like to grow up in my parents' household brings a mixed bag of thoughts and emotions. Jerry Lynn Presley was the son of a Baptist preacher, a husband, a dad, and a guy that others gravitated toward. He was a hard-working, incredibly affable man whom people loved. His quick wit and charisma drew people to him in almost any setting. Early in my life, my dad was not around much. He was a cross-country trucker, hauling mail from Memphis to Los Angeles on a weekly route. I can remember seeing him off on Sunday afternoons with my mom and sister and then welcoming him home the following Friday. He almost always brought us a surprise when he returned, and he would look to make up for lost time on Saturdays as much as possible, but to a large degree, the first ten-to-twelve years of my life were spent with an absent father. That said, there is no doubt that I learned the basic art of sales from my dad, as well as the value of hard work and a job well done.

When he was at home, he did what he could to make up for being gone so much. My most fond memories of my childhood revolve around time spent with him fishing and camping. Our family would go camping, usually with another family or two, so those were fun times, albeit not an activity that really got in my blood as something I wanted to continue later in life. Think about it, why sleep outside in a damp tent where there are perfectly good hotels available anywhere we want to go? But fishing was just between me and my dad. We would run trotlines and jugs and fish from our little aluminum boat. All to land that big, elusive catfish. To secure the bait to fish with, we would seine small ponds by putting on muck boots and wading around the periphery of these snake-ridden little mud pits. He would pull one side while I the other, and once we traversed the pond in its entirety, we would pull the net out and check our spoils. Lots of tadpoles, minnows, and crayfish accompanied by snakes and other nefarious types would fill those nets, and we would take the ones we needed and dump the rest back in the pond. It was an arduous task, but I loved every second of it. Once we pulled our prizes from the trotlines and jugs, we would clean those fish and a fish fry was on the horizon!

My dad was an Air Force man, and some of my favorite pictures of him are in uniform. Well before my sister or I came along, he was stationed in both Japan and Hawaii. I remember an old trunk in our attic (before the house burned and we lost most everything in said attic) that held military memorabilia, particularly from his stint in Japan. Looking back, we have marveled at the uncanny resemblance between my dad and *cousin* Elvis. Elvis falls solidly into the spot of eighth cousin for me, but we like to joke that my dad was actually Elvis' twin brother separated at birth. They were the same age, looked eerily alike, and were from generally the same region in the south, so hey, why not? But I digress. Other than a few trinkets and a smattering of pictures, I don't know much about his military career.

He never really spoke about it, and I took that to mean that he wasn't interested in reliving whatever that experience brought into his life. My dad could talk with the best of them, but there was always a side of him that was distant and seemed to be off-limits, and his military career lived in that space.

I mentioned that he was the son of a Southern Baptist preacher. Following in his dad's footsteps was never on the table for my dad. In fact, it was often the topic of conversation around family gatherings that I would be the next Presley in the pulpit. As of yet, that has not proven to be God's plan for me, but never say never! My dad was a good man, a man who became a true Christian later in life, but occupying a space in ministry was not anything he ever considered. I'm thankful for his roots, and I still have many of my grandfather's handwritten sermons from the 1940s and 1950s; I hold them as some of my most prized possessions.

From a career standpoint, my dad was again a mixed bag. As mentioned, for the first ten-plus years of my life, he traveled the country in a big rig, and he loved that life. That all changed when he made a run to Chicago, slipped on an icy step, and fell and ruptured several vertebrae in his lower back. His subsequent fusion surgery was somewhat botched, ending his career on the road and beginning a time as a self-proclaimed entrepreneur. He opened a self-serve laundromat and sold fresh fruit and vegetables in downtown Brownsville from the back of a trailer, among a few other attempted and failed business ventures, until he landed in the used car business. This business is what I remember most about my dad's career as it began in late middle school for me and continued until he was forced into early retirement due to his failing health.

The car business brought a new spin to my relationship with my dad. I would travel with him to auto auctions around the Mid-South, and those were fun times for me. I developed a love for cars that I carry to this day, and along that path, I purchased and titled over fifty cars to call my own. I stopped counting at fifty, and that was many years ago, so who knows what that actual number is today. I was exposed to some things where I might have been better served if I had been a bit older than I was at the time, but my time following my dad around the used car auction circuit was an education by any means.

The week after I turned sixteen, we drove down to Houston, TX, to purchase a truckload of cars to be shipped back. We bought more than the truck could carry, so I drove one the entire ten-hour trip home, not even a week after securing my license. Live and learn, as they say! We spent more and more time together, both on the road and at our car lot. He opened three different locations over the next few years, and I developed my own side business of car detailing for the public when I was not cleaning his cars from the lot. I learned the value of being meticulous in a task, and the outcomes drove my business for me. This taught me quite a bit about the value of hard work and discipline toward a job well done, something I carry with me to this day.

During our travels together going to auto auctions around the region, I soon became the official buyer for our business. Normally it took some time for the auctioneers to take this young kid seriously as a bidder, but that wasn't always the case. Once there was a gold Pontiac Trans Am that came through, and since my dad was not around, I proceeded to step up and win the bidding, ultimately paying quite a bit more than the car was worth. Needless to say, my dad was not happy, and we eventually lost money on that purchase. That was a hard lesson to learn but yet another one that stuck with me: be careful of the lure of those things that appeal to you but might not be worth the price.

I mentioned earlier that I learned some of the basic principles of sales from my dad. Better stated, I learned how to sell by watching him interact with his customers on our car lots. I learned a priceless nugget that I carry today, one that I will argue with the most accomplished sales leaders in the world if they are foolish enough to disagree with me. One of the pivotal keys to sales success is based on one word: *relationships*. Yes, there are countless other factors, but without the rapport of an honest, transparent relationship, you will not find success along this path. That might seem out of place in the world of used car sales, but I once again beg to differ. I watched him gain the customers' trust through humor and honesty, and our business thrived. It wasn't long before I was not only buying but also selling, and I knew I had found my niche.

My dad was both easygoing and a hard disciplinarian. I realize that sounds like an oxymoron, but it was the crux of the man he was. From the public view, everyone loved my dad and his easygoing demeanor. He could talk to a wall, and he had a quick sense of humor, at least in his own opinion. He drove the team bus to Friday night football games when I was young and did the same for one of the mission trips I took with my youth group in high school. From all outward appearances, he was the cool dad and had it all together. More privately, he was incredibly strict. In my younger days, it was perfectly normal to use a belt or a twig to punish anything perceived as a violation of his conduct standards, and I will admit that I was on the receiving end of those more than once! *Yes, sir, no, ma'am, please,* and *thank you* were paramount in his belief system, and these became the standard within our household. I never had a problem with that as I view it as a common courtesy for those of us born and raised in the South. His expectations were always clear, and he was quick to act punitively, when necessary, all in his frame of mind to raise us in the best way he knew how.

College came and went, with not an abundance of interaction between me and my dad other than on holidays. My dad stayed busy, but he did not practice healthy habits. He was a smoker from the age of fourteen, and over the years that took quite a toll on his heart, lungs, and body. He endured multiple heart surgeries and suffered a couple of strokes, but he kept on fighting. His deteriorating health caused an early retirement, so later in life, he had more time on his hands. He filled this sitting around different locations in Brownsville, sipping coffee, shooting the breeze with the locals, and yes, smoking cigarettes. Remember my comment about deteriorating health? Those cigarettes were his primary cause. That habit caused multiple heart attacks and strokes in his life, weakening him to where he passed away at the fairly young age of seventy due to complications from his chronic conditions. We had the opportunity to tell him goodbye, and when he was removed from the respirator, he never took another breath, thus going on to be with his Savior.

DEVELOPING DAD

I've mentioned multiple times that he did the best he could in raising me. There were plenty of good times to offset his absence and disciplinarian style, and I never doubted that he loved me. I can't recall ever hearing him actually *say* those words to me, and he was not an affectionate type to offer hugs for comfort . . . or greetings. He never saw me play a tennis match, and even though he always wanted me to be a doctor, I think he would be proud of the man I became and the professional success I have enjoyed. It was a different time when I grew up, and I learned a lot from my dad, one of the resounding themes being that I always had to stand up for myself and those who can't stand for themselves, no matter the situation. That requires a boldness that wasn't an innate trait of mine, but he helped me develop that ability, maybe to an extreme which has followed me all of my life.

Needless to say, my relationship with my dad had a huge impact on how I chose to mold myself into that same role. Because of some of his styles and preferences, I chose to go the opposite direction, probably being more affectionate to my kids than they prefer and making it a point to always tell them how much I love them time and time again. It has been my desire to not only never miss an event where my kids performed but to almost always even be a part of, or at a minimum be an observer at, their practices leading up to such events. Most of us want something better for our kids than we had for ourselves, whether it be stronger financial stability, more love, more involvement, more opportunities, and the list goes on. For me, I learned so much from my dad, both good and bad, and I only want to be better for my family in every single way I possibly can. My dad did the best he could, and I continue to do the same. I loved my dad, and nearly twenty years after he passed away, I still harbor great memories of how I was raised. I pray my kids will take my efforts and go forward in a better way as well, just as I continue to strive to do in their lives. In the end, no one gets it all right, but we sure can give it our best shot and know that the Lord will take our best efforts and do great things for our future generations. That is and forever will be, a noble calling.

Trudi's Dad

Simply put, to know Trudi's dad was to love him. He was humble, selfless, kind, faithful, and quiet in his own way. Truly a servant leader who always put others ahead of himself, a man who gave unconditional love while protecting and providing for his family. I have never met a man more affable and loving, more patient and kind—a man who was truly honorable and loved.

Admittedly I don't know as much of his history as I do my own dad. I didn't meet him until I was in college. But even knowing that, allow me to tell you a little about that story . . . .

The year was 1990, and I was a junior in college. His name was Charles Montgomery, known to most simply as Mr. Charlie. When I met him, Mr. Charlie was a fifty-six-year-old soap salesman for the Dial Corporation. Yes, I said soap salesman, and let me tell you, I would come to learn that this too can be a noble calling.

Mr. Charlie was always quick with a smile, a handshake, a pat on the back . . . and a story. In particular he loved to tell stories about his childhood. He loved baseball, and to hear him tell it, he was quite good at it. He was a die-hard St. Louis Cardinals fan and could tell you anything you wanted to know about them, past or present. But when he was in the eighth grade, everything changed. At the age of fourteen, his dad passed away unexpectedly. Young Charles immediately dropped out of school to take over working on the family farm. He took the everyday responsibilities of the farm and family on his shoulders for the next few years. Needless to say, he learned what hard work was all about.

At the ripe age of nineteen, he married his eighteen-year-old sweetheart. They slipped across the state line into Mississippi where that was actually normal at that time to be wed at such a young age. Out of his dedication to the farm and family, they stayed close to his mom for some time, both taking jobs in a local factory to help provide for themselves and others. In the late 1950s, Mr. Charlie started his career in sales. He was a perennial "salesman of the month" with the Star Coffee Company, and early in his career, he learned and exemplified what I now call the three rules of sales success:

1. Outwork your competition.
2. Observe and obey the Golden Rule.
3. Your word is your bond.

Mr. Charlie never actually sat me down and laid out this three-point guide for me, but I picked it up from my time with him and simply by how he lived his life. I didn't know it at the time, but those three guidelines would shape my career more than anything I would learn in college. I also found that by applying these concepts in every aspect of my life I could accomplish more and make a bigger difference in this big world we all call home.

Moving forward, Mr. Charlie and his bride had two sons, and these two guys both shared his love for baseball. Oh, and by the way, he took a new job, this one with the Dial Corporation. Yes, the same company he was with when I met him in 1990. The thing was, in order to work for this company, a high school diploma was required. If you recall, Mr. Charlie dropped out of school in the eighth grade to take care of his family. So in 1970, at the age of thirty-six, he passed his GED exam and started a job with the last company he would ever work for.

A year later in 1971, Mr. Charlie's life improved in a way he could never quite put into words. That statement in and of itself sheds some light on the magnitude of this development, as I have already told you that he loved a great story and could tell them with the best of them. But this was different. This was the year his third child was born, his baby girl who was indeed the apple of his eye. His love for her was palpable, and he just had a different gleam in his eye when he talked about her. Life was good.

So let's get back to where we started in 1990. Fast-forward from there and take the leap with me to 1992. It is Wednesday night, February 5th, 1992. I went to see Mr. Charlie and his bride, Ms. Thelma, at their house with big intentions. Right there, sitting at their kitchen table, I asked them for their permission to marry their baby girl. Yes, that is my wife, Trudi, whom you have already been introduced to and have most likely already fallen in love with, just like I did. Ten months later, Mr. Charlie walked her down the aisle, and I promised him to love her, to honor her, and to always take care of her. I have now been blessed with over thirty-one years of marriage with Mr. Charlie's baby girl, the apple of his eye who changed his life forever, and guess what? The same statement serves as an *understatement* in my own life.

But his story doesn't end there. In September of 1997, Mr. Charlie was diagnosed with non-Hodgkin's lymphoma. This was just after our first child, Lauren, was born, and that was just what Mr. Charlie needed to live for. You see, Lauren was Mr. Charlie's sixth grandchild (remember Trudi's brothers?), but she was the first *granddaughter*. And just like that, Mr. Charlie had a *new* apple of his eye. My favorite picture of him to this day is from a victory lap where he carried Lauren in his arms during a Relay for Life event, celebrating remission from this devastating disease.

However, in the winter of 1999, his cancer came back with a vengeance. Trudi was pregnant with Cam, Mr. Charlie's seventh grandchild and sixth grandson. Mr. Charlie held on until Cam was born in March. He spent the last nine weeks of his life in the hospital, with his bride by his side for every single minute. He went to be with the Lord a few short weeks after he held my son for the first time, a true testament to the power of the human spirit. Mr. Charlie would have loved my boy, an incredibly accomplished shortstop in baseball and a state champion in tennis as we have already discussed. We didn't even know what hospice was back then, but oh, how I wish we had! I'll never forget the nurse wheeling him into Trudi's delivery room where he first held Cam, and that grin we all knew and loved from Mr. Charlie returned one more time.

Fast-forward to July of 2019. Mr. Charlie's bride, my mother-in-law, Mrs. Thelma, passed away peacefully in her sleep at the age of eighty-four. A wonderful woman and a testament to a life well-lived. As we worked through their estate, we discovered something pretty amazing. Look at this: Mr. Charlie, who had passed away some twenty years earlier, who was a middle-school dropout who got his GED in his mid-thirties and never made a huge annual salary, who never even got to meet his eighth grandchild, his second granddaughter, our Emma—that incredible man had set up an account for his grandkids which proved to be an amazing blessing to them. At Thanksgiving in 2019 at our annual family gathering, we were able to present a check to each of the eight grandkids in the amount of ten thousand dollars each, and that was aside from the inheritance for his own three kids. Now this is not at all about the money—not one bit; rather, it is about a life well-lived and a legacy of doing the right thing and loving people. The difference he made in the lives of his kids, his grandkids, and yes, in my own life, are quite frankly incalculable in my opinion. What a legacy! Learn from Mr. Charlie the way I did. A life well-lived is what defines your legacy.

Me

I'm a lot. I know it, and I fully admit it. I think it is OK to be a lot, as long as you have the self-awareness to see it, own it, and admit it. Maybe for others, it isn't quite that simple, but I embrace who I am, warts and all.

To most who know me, I would appear to be confident, maybe even cocky at times. I joke with others that the only person in this world who is allowed to actually call me cocky is my wife, simply because if anyone has ever earned the right to do so, it is her. But appearances can sometimes be deceiving.

Just because I may appear confident doesn't mean it is the truth. To be transparent, I struggle probably more than most with my confidence. I am the classic embodiment of a phenomenon called *imposter syndrome,* a condition where one never feels he is worthy or capable of the title or status he holds. I question myself constantly: *Am I making a mistake by doing this or that? Am I really giving good advice to my kids? Am I modeling what a good husband looks like? Do I even know what I am doing at work? Am I good enough? Am I smart enough or am I just a fraud trying to get through the day?* I think every bit of that speculation has roots and some truth but not in totality. Those things do not define me, do not cause me sleepless nights, and do not keep me from getting out of bed each day to do it all over again. Do I struggle? Of course. You probably do too, at least in some areas of your life. But do my struggles define me? Absolutely not!

If asked to define myself, I would say I am a believer, I am a husband, I am a dad. Those are my cornerstones. I tend at times to let my job define me; but hear me on this—that is a mistake *every single time.* Do not allow your job to define you or cause you to live in fear or angst. Unless you own your own business, I assure you that if you left your job today, your company would move on immediately and have your position posted before the door closed behind you. Root yourself firmly in who and what makes you stronger and brings you joy. I told you how I would define myself; what about you?

In some ways, I would appear to be successful. In just as many others, I would appear to be an abject failure. But how am I measured as a dad? None of us are classically trained on how to be a great dad. If you are reading this book, most likely you are at least interested in being a good dad or maybe even improving upon your current position as a dad. I openly share my mistakes as well as my wins as a dad in the hope that someone, *anyone*, will learn a tiny lesson from me and take a giant leap in their dad journey.

I firmly believe that God put me on this earth to have a positive impact in the lives of others. Those "others" most entrusted to me would be Trudi, Lauren, Cam, and Emma. Now we can add Glori to this limited list, as we have welcomed her into our inner circle and love her like she is our own. Each of these amazing people would tell you that I've made mistakes along the way, probably more mistakes than the things I actually got right. But it is my most sincere desire that each of them know that no matter what, I always have and I always will love them unconditionally. I try to lead, whether at home or work, with a style that is motivational, inspirational, and transformational. But what does that really mean?

To me, being motivational is important because everyone can benefit from a motivated stance in life. Motivation is a constant effort, however, as it is frighteningly fleeting. One must continually go to the well and share the refreshing water of motivation to help others start off right and get on the right track with their mindset. Did I mention that motivation is fleeting? That is where the next phase becomes necessary.

Inspiration has a bit more grit. By this I mean it has some sticktoitiveness, even though I don't think that is a real word. If you inspire someone, you have given them a platform to go out there and motivate others, thus creating a more perpetual cycle of helping others with their mindset. An inspirational leader truly impacts others in a more lasting manner, so why not start with that at home?

I'm sure my family will laugh at this section, even if they won't do so to my face. They know my strategies and tactics that I use to lead my work teams and have more than once balked at me when I attempted to use said approach on them. Whether it was our failed attempts at "family meetings" or a quote I would throw out to them, I usually got at least an eye roll out of it at home, mainly because they knew they could get away with it. I can't begin to tell you how many times we would be together at a movie, listening to a sermon, at a game, or even watching something on TV when we would witness something inspirational, and one of them would turn to me and say, "I bet you're going to use that, aren't you?" You know what? Every single time they were correct! Motivation leads to inspiration, which in turn leads to transformation.

    If you are a transformational leader, you are certainly making a difference out there. By definition, to *transform* means to make a thorough or dramatic change. That word *thorough* is impactful to me, and I take that to mean it is through and through. When one changes thoroughly, real impact has been achieved and a lifetime of positive development is possible. No matter where you currently sit in your role as a father or a leader, transformational change should be on your agenda. It is not something you can simply declare and conquer. It is a time-honoring process and a process in which you never really arrive. My teams often hear me say, "The finish line is our starting point." That can certainly apply to goals and objectives, but more importantly, it means that this quest to be a transformational leader is a lifelong quest, one that requires consistent study and observation, and application through trial and error is without a doubt part of the process. My family might half-heartedly make fun of me for my approach to this, but if in any way I have succeeded in being a transformational influence in each of their lives, then I consider it mission accomplished.

    What does all of this mean to you, a dad looking to be the best dad possible? I mentioned a bit ago that I have made many mistakes, but the key is to learn from those mistakes, particularly as the dad you are. I often say that there is only one Trent Presley out there and that we should all be thankful for that! Truly, God did make all of us in a unique fashion, and that is why, at least in my opinion, there is no template, no workbook, no study guide where you can simply adopt everything that someone else did and come out successfully on the other side of yourself. It is taking bits and pieces of what we learn from others, molding it into the best version of how it fits into the puzzle of your life, and then making it solely your own. Again, that is a never-ending process, so buckle in and prepare yourself for the ride of your life—the journey to be the dad you were designed to be.

In the end, I try, and I try, and I try. I will never stop trying. I will never stop trying to honor my wife with my words, thoughts, and actions. I will never stop trying to simply be there for her and for our kids. I will never stop trying to lead a life that makes them proud. Proud of me as Trudi's husband and our kids' dad, proud of the effort I put into their development, and proud of the relationship that we continue to have today. As Lauren, Cam, and Emma get further into adulthood, it is my prayer they will know how deeply I truly love them and that even though I failed so often, I always wanted to be the perfect version of the dad they wanted and deserved. I will never live up to the standard I set for myself, but I will not stop trying. A simple word of advice for you as the reader: **don't stop trying**.

Chapter 10

FAITH & TRUST

It is no secret that I love Disney. I love going to Orlando to experience the craziness of the Walt Disney World parks and resorts. I love the crowds, I love the customer service, I love the experience in general. Oddly enough, as I write this chapter, I am sitting on the deck of a treehouse in Monteagle, TN, listening to a nearby rooster crow as the sun attempts to break the dawn—quite peaceful and quite the opposite of an early morning scene rushing to a rope drop at one of the Disney parks! But I digress, so back to this particular topic.

When the kids were young, I didn't love waiting in lines to meet the characters. Oh, we took some great photos with the princesses and what they referred to as the "fuzzy characters," but I don't believe I could count the hours we spent waiting on those characters and that elusive signature they would add to their souvenir books.

Another line I have never been a huge fan of is the one for the Peter Pan ride. With all of the great rides throughout the Magic Kingdom, that Peter Pan ride always remains one of the longest wait times in the park. Here's a little secret: *it's not worth it.* Sure, it's cute and whimsical, and if you could walk right on it would be great. But with wait times sometimes soaring past the two-hour mark, nah, just not worth it. A line from the original *Peter Pan* movie sparks the title of this chapter, however, and while I will take on a bit of a different spin, I share with you that all it takes is a little "faith, trust, and pixie dust."

Admittedly I will forego much on the aforementioned pixie dust. Not sure what that is other than it allows the characters in the movie to fly when they are lacking in the faith and trust departments. Maybe we all do need a dose of that special dust at times in our lives just to remind us of what really matters and that Someone is always right there with us to help us along our path. If so, take that little nugget with you, and maybe you can be the living embodiment of that certain someone. Faith and trust, though interrelated, can be all too elusive for so many of us in the hustle and bustle of our lives.

Faith. As a Christian, my thoughts go immediately to our faith in Jesus Christ, my Savior and Redeemer. And I tell you, that's the right place to start, but it is also more than that in a family unit. Faith is something that you must develop in each other. Faith that no matter what, you are there for one another. In Hebrews 11, faith is defined as "being sure of what we hope for and certain of what we do not see." Yep, that's it, and as simple as it may sound to take that proverbial leap of faith, when that leap is into an abyss that you have no clue how to traverse, you need someone there beside you to take your hand and leap with you. That is where your family comes into play. We have had to take leaps of faith as a family due to circumstances in our lives, most likely all of us have. But knowing they were right there with me always made those leaps a little easier.

Faith is not something you can conjure up; it is not something that you can fabricate. By its very definition, it is being sure of all things unsure, and maybe even for no apparent or rational reason. I tell you this: without faith, not only is your life less full, but your future is most certainly in jeopardy. Which leads me to trust.

Trust. This is not something that comes easily to me. By nature, I *was* a trusting guy. Note the word *was*. But life can cause cynicism to creep in and rob you of that ability to trust others. While I am thankful that has never been the case with my family, it has ruled the day in my professional life, causing me to keep people at arm's length most of the time. To a fault, almost any time I allow myself to trust someone or some circumstance at work, I am betrayed or let down in some fashion. As a result, trust is no longer something I freely give; rather, it is something that must be earned. Maybe that is not a bad stance to take anyway, but when you are forced down that path, it cements itself and becomes an almost unbreakable barrier. Trust, however, is essential in your family unit, so let me walk down that path with you.

Who do you trust? If you ask me that question, my immediate and unequivocal answer would be my wife, Trudi. She has never once been anything but honest and forthright with me, and I do indeed trust her with my life. Do I trust my kids? You better believe it. Have there been times in their lives when they deceived me? The simple answer—*yes*. We encouraged an absolute open-door policy at our house as our kids were growing up with the promise that if they told the truth, all would be good. That didn't mean there would not necessarily be consequences, but we would be good. After all, every action has consequences, either good or bad, but we valued honesty and openness in all things and achieved a great cadence of these traits through the years.

As parents, you almost always know when there is deception or misdirection in play with your kids. I say *almost* because I am sure there have been times when I was fooled and they "got away with it." These are three of the best kids that have ever walked this earth, and I know their intentions were good, no matter the circumstance. I did the same thing as a kid, hiding events, not sharing all of the pertinent details, and completely ignoring the rules, all in an attempt to get by on something where I had chosen the wrong path. As with our kids, that usually didn't work out for me, but on that rare occasion when it did, I thought I was bullet proof! Usually, in time, whatever that was would come back around and bite me, and that was true with our kids as well.

Back to the relationship between faith and trust. While faith cannot be seen, trust can be defined as a firm belief in the reliability, truth, ability, or strength of someone or something. They almost sound like opposites, but indeed they walk hand in hand. No, not even the combination of faith, trust, and pixie dust will allow you to actually fly, but the first two will allow you to fly free, to live a little bit lighter, to not worry so much about what might lie around the corner—simply stated, to live a life of peace. We must all surround ourselves with people in whom we have faith and trust.

As a dad, I believe it is my responsibility to foster the environment of these traits in my home so that my kids always have a *safe place*. A place of sanctuary; a place where the truth could be spoken without fear of judgment; a place where no matter what, they know they are loved and appreciated. It is my prayer that by modeling this in our home, as they go and establish their own lives and families they will foster a similar environment so their kids will experience this same kind of openness and support. Does it take hard work? Yes! Does it take that "leap of faith" to achieve trust? Yes! Will there be times when you feel alone and like everyone is out to get you? Yes! But if you have that established faith in the Lord, faith in your family, and trust that creates a tie that binds, you will never walk alone.

As I look back on my continuing journey of faith and trust, one recurring event stands out in the development of my relationship with my kids: **bedtime prayers**. I'm not sure of the specific date when this started as a physical event with each of them, but those few minutes every evening with each of them have proven to be priceless to me. You already know that Trudi and I prayed for and prayed over our kids before they were even born, and if you are not doing that even today with your kids—no matter what their age—start right now. The physical act of kneeling beside their bed each night and having a time of prayer for and with your kids is an experience like none other. To hear their sweet prayers as little kids, and for them to hear you earnestly pray for every aspect within their lives is beyond anything that you can comprehend. I do not know if they looked forward to that time as much as I did, but even on the nights when I was maybe not as dialed in as I should have been, I always emerged from their rooms feeling blessed. Take the time to pray for and pray with your kids. Their takeaways will be innumerable, not the least of which is building implicit trust that you are there for them and you love them beyond anything that might occur in life or anything you could ever possess.

FAITH & TRUST

Faith, trust, and pixie dust. Nothing magical about it, but at the same time nothing is more important than those first two in the development of a solid family unit. Take that blind leap of *faith* as you invest in your familial relationships, and *trust* that when you leap, the net will appear.

Chapter 11

WINNING AND LOSING

It is my freshman year in high school, and the day has arrived for my first official tennis match. This is my first attempt at this sport, as I had played football and basketball at my prior school, both with limited accolades to say the least. But I had found something in this sport called tennis, a sport known as a "country club" sport, which certainly didn't fit me or my socioeconomic upbringing or status in the community. We were the prototypical blue-collar, working-class family, so why did I think I could play tennis? I can't answer that other than to say that when I transferred schools, I knew I would not be playing football or basketball any longer, so I was introduced to tennis.

Back to that fateful day in the spring of 1984. I'm the number three seed of the mighty Haywood High Tomcats, and we have traveled to that powerhouse tennis school in Newbern, TN, the Dyer County Choctaws. I stepped out of my 1980 Mazda R-X7, fully confident I was about to get my first win of my high school career. If memory serves correctly, they had four courts, so I was one of the first ones on. My opponent had yet to step on the court, so I walked close to the net and began hitting a ball into it just to get loose. I took a bigger-than-necessary forehand swing and somehow managed to overswing, and I popped myself right in the head with my racket! I was embarrassed, so I took a quick look around, relieved that no one seemed to have noticed, escaping further humility . . . or so I thought.

I went back to my swings into the net, albeit a bit lighter this round, when I felt something trickle down my face. If you have ever played spring high school tennis in Tennessee, you know I wasn't sweating as that season starts out frigidly cold. I reached up and wiped my face, only to pull my hand away to find it covered in blood. Yes, *my* blood! I had popped open a cut on my forehead that Mick couldn't have closed in the ring for Rocky Balboa. It was actually right in my eyebrow, and I was bleeding like a stuck pig right there on the court. My opponent had just arrived, and he just stared at me like I had two heads. I told him I'd be right back, so I went and found my coach who proceeded to basically smear my blood across the rest of my face and put a bandage on my eyebrow and told me to go play. As people gathered around the fence to watch, not in awe of my amazing tennis prowess but rather wondering what in the world was wrong with this guy, I proceeded to dispatch my opponent by a score of 8-3. A couple of hours later, I made it to the emergency room to get seven stitches, and a real legend was born.

Well, not really. I did go on to have a decent high school career, earning a top-twenty-five ranking in my state and earning a partial scholarship to a small college, but none of it ever really lived up to the drama of my bloody first match that cold spring day way back then.

You see, life can be misconstrued as being about winning and losing. We see this application in sports every day. We also see it in our jobs, in politics, even in religion. I've heard it said that we never really lose, we just learn. While those lessons are important, I don't prescribe to that notion at all. There is always a scoreboard, and someone is always watching. We do learn from our losses, otherwise we are no better than the animals that return to the same trap. Hopefully we celebrate wins and move on from the losses, but that is sometimes easier said than done. What is more important than all of these lessons we can learn from life and sports? *Perseverance.*

The ability to hang on when you're barely hanging in. It would have been easy to walk off the tennis court when I had blood streaming down my face and hope to live to fight another day, but even as a skinny, immature kid, that was not who I was. I like the word *sticktoitiveness* that I used a few pages before. It summarizes the old adage—*When the going gets tough, the tough get going*—all in one made-up word. I don't claim to be some tough guy, not by any means, but on the things that matter to me most, you simply will not win. I love this quote by actor Will Smith, taken from an interview with Tavis Smiley on June 17, 2011:

> *The only thing that I see that is distinctly different about me is I'm not afraid to die on a treadmill. I will not be outworked, period. You know? You might have more talent than me, you might be smarter than me, you might be sexier than me, you might be all of those things, you got it on me in nine categories. But if we get on the treadmill together . . . there's two things: You're getting off first, or I'm going to die. It's really that simple. . . . You're not going to out-work me.*[1]

That, my friends, is perseverance. We all want to win, there is no denying that, but victory is *more* than winning. Victory goes to those who are tenacious, sometimes a little obstinate, diligent, truthful, fair, respectful, positive, gregarious, caring, confident, yet humble and pure of heart. You see, there is a path to winning, and doing it the right way is always the best way!

So according to the scoreboard, it does remain true: life is about winning and losing . . . but not really. If you choose to persevere, if you choose to not quit, if you choose to walk the path less traveled, if you are willing to outwork everyone else—abide by this simple yet difficult formula, and you will win. Period.

---

1. Quote from Will Smith, in an interview with Tavis Smiley on June 17, 2011, https://www.youtube.com/watch?v=VH6mPeQfRLY. Used with permission from TS Media, Inc.

Chapter 12

TURN THE PAGE . . .

If you have ever walked through a cow pasture, one thing is exceedingly evident—you must watch each and every step you take. While this might be a somewhat crude visual, I think you get the point. We must carefully choose each step we take in life and be prepared; there will be obstacles in your *dad walk* that cause you to stumble. Proverbs 24:16 states, "For a righteous man falls down seven times, and rises again." My interpretation of that is, "Fall down seven times, get up eight." As a dad, we fall. It is part of our infallible human experience—simply a fact of life. In reality, it isn't about how often we fall or even how hard we fall. It is the fact that we get back up and go again. This is where I will introduce what I call *turn-the-page moments*. Allow me to unpack this further with you.

There are instances in life where things just don't go our way. I think back to when our kids walked a dark path, a time of uncertainty, confusion, sadness, or just being scared. These are the times when, as a dad, you must shine above all others. As referenced, I call them *turn-the-page moments*, and what I mean by that is this: As their dad, someone they put their full trust and faith in, you must be there with them when things do not go their way. Something seemingly monumental in their life that must be faced or overcome, all so that they can be assured that yes, indeed, the sun will come out tomorrow. It is your job to help them turn that page and know that God's plan for them is still in the works, that this too will pass, and you will be stronger for it. You do not have to be a hero. Face it, most of us would fail in comparison to whomever our kids claim to be their hero, but no matter what, you must stand tall and strong *with* them and *for* them when their world seems to shatter. Real life is always the best tutor, so here is a brief turn-the-page moment from each of our kids' lives.

For Lauren, it was that tennis match at Crockett County when she was in fifth grade. A match she should have easily won, but she didn't. She came off the court crying, and I didn't help one bit. Instead of simply hugging her and being there for her in silence, I immediately jumped into what she should have and could have done differently. It hurt her, and in the long run it hurt me as I realized my mistake. All she needed was for me to be there and hug her . . . in silence. I fell down, but I got back up, and I still remember that final hug seven years later on the court at the state tournament of her senior year. I simply hugged her in silence, and I cried with her. *Turn the page.*

Then there was what I'll call the boyfriend experience. In college, her relationship with a long-time friend blossomed into what appeared to be a storybook romance. We all thought this might just be the one, but God had a different plan for Lauren. It was another difficult experience in her life and by default in ours as well, but this became the epitome of a turn-the-page moment in her life, and Lauren grew incredibly strong through the pain and difficulty of a breakup that none of us saw coming. Again, as her dad it was simply my job to be there. To be silent and be present. You see, Lauren taught me how to wait as a dad. I owe that growth in my own life to her. She taught me that everything isn't about an immediate takeaway or a lesson to be learned. Sometimes the situation dictates that you just *be. Be* there, *be* silent, *be* supportive, *be* her dad. Lauren is one of the strongest people I know, and I admire her more than she could ever know. Her strength and resiliency inspire me, but even the strong need support, and I will always be that support for her when she needs it. Without a doubt, she turned the page and is living her life in a way that many others only wish they could. *Turn the page.*

As we have discussed, Cam played so many sports that there was a myriad of times where I fell as his dad. But one in particular stands out. We were at practice—yes, I said practice—and Cam was just having a bad day on the field. He missed a throw from short to first, then he missed again, and then he missed yet again. For whatever reason, I lost my mind and yelled at him in front of his teammates as well as the parents who were present at practice. It wasn't just that I yelled at him; I embarrassed him. I pulled him off the field and made him sit in the dugout, all the while I'm still ranting about his mistakes.

Guess what? They were *just mistakes,* and I had no right to treat him that way. After practice, I realized the error of my ways, and that evening as we retired to Cam's room to pray before bed, I offered him maybe the sincerest apology I have ever issued. He deserved that and more, and to his credit, he forgave me. But I never forgot how I hurt my ten-year-old son that day. So yes, I fell down, but I got back up and kept going, mostly because that little guy chose to forgive me. *Turn the page.*

Of course, there was a girlfriend experience worth recounting. High school romances are exciting, fresh, fun, and sometimes . . . devastating. Cam and his high school girlfriend made a beautiful couple, but as his parents, Trudi and I never had much confidence in a real future for them. Cam has an incredible heart, and he was there to help his friends and his girlfriend with anything they might need. As it turned out, there were needs as it would be with any teenage girl and their friends of that age. They were a good couple, but when it ended it was a difficult blow. It was the timing as much as anything, as Cam had just come off winning the state championship in tennis and decided not to play in college, so his tennis identity had come to a close. That same week he and his girlfriend broke up, so that part of his identity ended as well. That caused him great angst, and I remember sitting upstairs with this six-foot-two, strong young man and holding him as he cried through the pain of change and uncertainty. This was a turn-the-page moment for Cam, and he became stronger through it as well. I admire him with the stance that only a proud dad can feel, and I look up to him in so many ways that I lost count long ago. Strength and character define him, and I know what a great dad he will one day be. *Turn the page.*

I've mentioned before that Emma was the beneficiary of me learning from my mistakes with Lauren and Cam. With that said, I can confidently say that I didn't make any mistakes with Emma as she grew up. *[Dramatic pause.]* I can't even write that with a straight face! One would think after the countless times I messed up with her siblings that I would have it figured out for her, but that would be an incorrect assumption. Emma's love and dedication to cheer pushed her to the top of the heap in her sport, and her dedication to it equated to near flawless performances throughout her cheer career. But the final product, in this case each performance at the competitions, does not always paint the full picture. There were countless mornings leading up to competition that were anything but harmonious. The diva side of cheer would emerge in those hotel rooms around the country and some all-out battles would ensue. We saw a different side of our sweet little girl during the prep for those competitions.

Once again, enter dad as the enforcer. On more than one occasion, I would treat Emma in less than a respectful manner as I corrected her attitude on what I like to call "game day." Correction is not wrong in and of itself, but my mannerisms, my speech, my attitude, and my delivery went too far more than once. Something about those experiences just pushed my buttons, and I had enough. I cornered Emma in some nameless hotel and laid into her about her attitude and threatened to not even let her take the floor that day. Stupid threats, as I would have never done that to her or her team, but I allowed myself to go too far. I see Emma crying as a result of my anger being directed at her, and it breaks my heart to this day. Again, I learned from this mistake eventually, and I can't help but think again of those happy times in her car as she and I sang our versions of carpool karaoke together . . . and all was good. *Turn the page.*

As I think about Emma and her turn-the-page moments, it reminds me of experiences with Lauren and Cam. Cheer had been Emma's passion for half of her entire life, and when it ended, it became her turn-the-page moment. It was devastating for her to leave behind the comfort of the familiar, a place where she excelled and was a proven leader and face the next phase of her life with great unknowns to come. I remember this moment as well, in Orlando, FL, when she came off the stage for the last time. I held her as she wept, releasing all of her fears and uncertainties, and not yet knowing this was a turn-the-page moment for her. I am so proud of how she moved forward, putting the past behind, forging a path toward her future, and becoming another in the line of the Presley kids who is strong and valiant in her resolve and her dedication to find what comes next. To say I am proud is an understatement of epic proportions, and her strength and determination are just two of her qualities that make me beam with pride! *Turn the page.*

Perspective is my favorite word. People who know me best have heard me say this time and time again. Perspective is seeing things from the broader view, and when you think through pitfalls, perspective leads to the application portion. Face it, we are all going to fail. Unfortunately, we are going to fail, fail, and fail some more. But we must learn to recognize our failures as opportunities for improvement. Opportunities to improve our approach, our reaction, and most importantly, our relationship with those we love the most. It is one thing to want this, to think this, to intend to do this. But hear me on this: **intention without application is worthless**. Deciding to do something and actually doing it are two very different things. Just because you *want* to be a better dad, you *want* to react better to those situations that push your buttons, you *want* to be the hero of your own story . . . just wanting does nothing to help you accomplish it. You must identify your areas of shortfall; determine what you need to do to improve, how to go about said improvement, and the timeline you hope to accomplish this in. Then take that first fateful step forward to improvement. That, my friends, is a plan to accomplish your goal.

Not all of these examples I have shared will apply to you, but some will hit very close to home as you read this. It is my hope by sharing these failures and these turn-the-page moments that you realize you are not alone and that there is a takeaway that will help you take that first small step toward a better version of the dad you are. *Turn the page. . . .*

Chapter 13

EMPTY *NEXT*ING

It could be apropos that this chapter happens to be number thirteen, as in some circles empty nesting is associated with bankruptcy. A time for travel and lavish expenditures as we explore the world and see what is out there just waiting for us. But no, that isn't how we choose to approach this new phase in life. Do Trudi and I have plans for travel and adventure together now that our kids have entered their own new phases of life? You better believe it! But I think we differ from many of our peers in our approach to this phase of life referred to as *empty nesting*. In fact, I will rename it and I'll call it *empty nexting*!

    I have vivid recollections of each child's move-in day for college. The excitement of everything new, the anticipation of what is to come, the nervousness of the unknown, and the trepidation that Trudi and I felt with each delivery. For the girls, the lead-up was quite eventful—a lot of purchases in preparation for decorating the perfect dorm room with the right themes and colors. For Cam, it was almost as simple as grabbing a sleeping bag and walking through the doors. In case you don't already know, I'll let you in on another tightly held secret: boys are much different from girls! How about that for a nugget of wisdom? I'll say there is no greater example of this than the pomp and circumstance of move-in day when they go off to college.

As always, for Lauren, it was our first chance at this. We spent the day on campus, all the way through what has been dubbed the "crying chapel" service—aptly named, I might add. As Trudi and I pulled away that evening, we both cried. We took the incredibly long journey back home, every bit of 4.7 miles, and felt the impact of how much our world had just been rocked. One down, two to go, and it did *not* bring us joy.

We arrived on campus for Cam's move-in day a couple of years later. Again, same trepidation and excitement but altogether different. We walk in his dorm room only to be greeted by a nice gathering of black mold percolating underneath his dorm room bed. Thankfully this was Cam's room and not one of the girls, as his amenities were far easier to repack and move to his new assignment. Once settled, we continued through the same routine, culminating with the "crying chapel" where we once again cried, got in our car for that arduous 4.7-mile trip back home, and realized . . . two down, one to go.

Then in a flash it was Emma's turn. We repeated the process of hunting and gathering and spending a tidy sum to prepare for her dorm decor. Move-in day was déjà vu all over again as we repeated the process we have already experienced twice before. Wash, rinse, repeat. Again, we arrived at the aforementioned "crying chapel" where we once again complied, cried, and tackled the long road home culminating at the end of that same 4.7-mile journey. However, this time was indeed different. Empty nesting had officially begun, and with that thought, Trudi *really* cried. Don't get me wrong, it hit me too, but I remember hugging Trudi to comfort her, and the ever-soothing words that came out of my mouth were as follows: "I think you are really only crying because now you know you are stuck with only me!" Obviously, there is some truth to that. Remember how I already told you that I am a lot? But in the end, it was a comment intended to make her laugh, and it hit the mark as she did so and softened the moment a bit. Indeed, our official next phase of life, commonly referred to as empty nesting, had begun. Empty *nexting* implies just that: what's next? Let the games begin!

EMPTY NEXTING

That said, it was a bit of a false start. Not long after Emma's freshman year had begun and she had moved on campus, Cam was planning his proposal, and part of that process was to vacate his apartment where he had lived the past couple of years with his buddies, thus moving home in preparation for his incredible and wonderful journey toward marriage. So we had a total of nine full weeks of empty nexting our first round through it. But make no mistake, we loved every second of Cam's move back home. Although empty nesting does bring the opportunity to reconnect, travel, and just slow down a bit, Trudi and I are in one accord that any and all of our kids are *always* welcome to come back home and will be welcomed with open arms.

I chose the play on words to turn *empty nesting* into *empty nexting* almost by mistake. I say almost because as I was writing this chapter, I had a typo replacing the "s" with the "x," and it struck me as a clever play on words. So it stuck! As I thought through this further, I loved the intonation that it creates even in print. It is completely *not* about anything being empty but altogether about what comes next. The beautiful, wonderful, completely unknown of what lies around the corner for us. Sure, there is travel and reconnecting, but I'm already beginning to understand and appreciate the value of quiet. Just plain quiet. We have lived in an incredibly fast-paced life for the entire duration of our kids' journey to adulthood, and we loved every single minute of it (*mostly*). But now we sometimes find ourselves just sitting quietly together, and I absolutely love it!

My job sometimes requires that I travel, but now more than ever if I can have Trudi tag along, that is exactly what we do. I am working diligently to make changes in my career path that limit my business travel away from home, partly because I want to be home with Trudi, partly because I never want her to feel lonely, and partly because it is just that time in my life where being at home more is exactly what I want. Our black lab Ace loves the slower pace we have established, not to mention the extra attention he gets as he rules over his kingdom that we call our backyard. Find the silver lining; sometimes it might hide from you, but it exists and is waiting. You just have to be intentional in your search. Remember: leap, and the net will appear.

Some people do indeed empty nest through extravagant and excessive travel and expenditures. Let me be clear that I applaud that, and I say to each his own. This is your time—time to reflect and enjoy said reflection while considering what comes next. For us it is our time to get closer, to have some fun, and as I mentioned, to just do nothing. We proudly make the claim that we are not *those* parents—those who couldn't wait to kick their kids out of the house and move on with their lives. You know who those parents are, and in fact, it might be you. If so, do not take my emphasis here as condemnation; rather, just take it as another example of how we are all created equal but different, and what a wonderful mixture of diversity that really is.

As a kindergarten teacher, Trudi still gets to celebrate spring break in her work. Recently during such a break when she was out of school, I took the week off as well. You might think we had a great trip planned, just the two of us off on another adventure. But no, that was not what we wanted to do. We had our very own staycation, one filled with eating wherever we wanted, a planned activity each day that was deemed fun or an adventure, and a lengthy list of to-do items that we wanted to accomplish around the house. It was one of the best weeks we have had in a long time, and we thoroughly enjoyed our time together, working side-by-side on our projects and taking our time throughout each day. We didn't finish everything on our to-do list, so I see more days just like this in our near future as well. You make your own experiences, no matter what they may be. So just be intentional and enjoy the ride.

Even though we do not see our kids every day, sometimes not for weeks or even months at a time, we have not and will not cease to pray for them. Trudi and I pray together every morning before heading out to work, and it is an honor to lift Lauren, Emma, Cam, and Glori up to the Lord each day. Sometimes we have a very specific prayer for each of them, depending on what they are facing or what lies ahead, while other times we simply ask for God's grace and mercy to abound in each of their lives. Let's face it, it can be a big scary world out there, but when we stay grounded in our faith, it helps us face each day with confidence and anticipation of greatness. Remember how we talked about faith and trust? Insert and apply here as well.

EMPTY NEXTING

As much as we miss our kids, we are filled with anticipation of the wonderful things the Lord has in store for them as they live their lives. Again, they will always have a place to come home to if they so desire. That simply will not change.

As I have established, there are different types of empty nesters out there. We choose to be empty *nexters*, full of anticipation of the great things to come. "Next time" is a short phrase I love as it intonates something great or something exciting, or maybe just something better or different! There is an old gospel song titled "Because He Lives," and it is one of my favorites. If you don't know it, Google it and take a listen. It is full of encouragement about facing tomorrow, no matter what tomorrow may hold. In the world of empty nesters, we tend to think of tomorrow with excitement until something shakes that thought process. No matter how you view this phase of life, no matter if you celebrate an empty house or curse the quiet it brings, no matter if you get busy living or get busy dying, you get to make it your own. Even if you celebrate your kids' departure, keep them close when you can, and continue to pray for them as they go lead their best lives possible. This chapter remains unfinished, and I find that to be quite exciting. My favorite Steven Curtis Chapman song was released way back in 1992, and I think these lyrics offer a nice perspective on the great adventure awaiting us during our empty *nexting* phase:

> ♪ *Started out this morning in the usual way*
> *Chasing thoughts inside my head*
> *I thought I had to do today*
> *Another time around the circle*
> *Try to make it better than the last*
> *I opened up the Bible*
> *And I read about me*
> *Said I'd been a prisoner*
> *And God's grace had set me free*
> *And somewhere between the pages*
> *It hit me like a lightning bolt*
> *I saw a big frontier in front of me*
> *And I heard somebody say "Let's go!"* ♪

DEVELOPING DAD

> ♪ *Saddle up your horses*
> *We've got a trail to blaze*
> *Through the wild blue yonder of God's amazing grace*
> *Let's follow our leader into the glorious unknown*
> *This is the life like no other, whoa whoa*
> *This is The Great Adventure* ♪

Hey, by the way, just in case you were wondering . . . *I sure do love the life I get to share with my wife!* Empty *nexting*: what a great adventure!

Chapter 14

SIDEWAYS

It was December of 2006, and it started like any other day. My sister was a single mom with two young children, working hard to provide the life for them that they deserved. Her seven-year-old son went to school that day as usual, but it wasn't long before he knew something wasn't right. He started experiencing some physical manifestations that were disturbing, so the school connected with his mom who then took him to the emergency room. Through a series of events and tests, he was eventually transported to St. Jude Children's Research Hospital in Memphis, TN, where the feared diagnosis was confirmed. He had leukemia, and he was in for the fight of his life. Not only was he going to have to fight, but so was his mom, his sister, and all of those involved in his life.

    I had never been to St. Jude before this time. The day after he was admitted, Trudi and I went to visit him, and I have to say it was somewhat overwhelming. As you attempt to process the meaning of his diagnosis, his treatment, and all that circulates around that, the first and only place you can go is to the Lord. Prayers for healing, prayers for understanding, prayers for strength, and the list goes on. I stepped away from his room in the ICU and wandered out into a courtyard to do just that—*pray*. Along that short journey, I observed kids in various stages of disease treatment, and it simply broke my heart. But here's the thing: while these kids' bodies might have been broken, their spirits certainly were not! I was amazed at the vigor with which I saw them tackle their treatments. The life that exuded from them as they ran around the complex, playing with each other, playing with the security personnel, and not letting their difficulties steal their joy. I continued into the courtyard and sat on a bench and simply cried. Not so much for the difficulties my nephew faced ahead but for the brokenness that exists in our world and the obstacles of the journey that he and his mom were about to embark on. They were not alone in this journey, but we knew it would not be easy.

This is an actual experience presenting an example of the reality of the difficulties we sometimes face in life. There was no fault in this diagnosis, no reason that made any sense, no fingers to point. Just an incredibly difficult reality that they had to embrace and forge through. I'm happy to report that in this specific scenario, after years of treatments and wonderful care, he is now a healthy young man living his life to the fullest. God is good all the time. I stand by that statement, even when our circumstances might not seem to reflect this truth.

Then of course, there is the dad, mom, husband, or wife who did everything right. They love each other. They love their kids. They treat each other with respect. They love the Lord. They teach their kids all the right lessons, all the right rules, all the right things. But then the wheels come off the track. They get that dreaded call where their child has been arrested—or worse, their child strays from the Lord, abandons church, makes lifestyle choices outside of the biblical parameters of how they were raised. Maybe these parents have educated their kids on the dangers of drugs and alcohol but still see failure in application in the lives of their kids. In some cases, these parents lose their kids to the world, and in others, tragically they lose them to death. No matter the loss, the pain and devastation are world-shattering for these parents. It can be overwhelming and utterly heartbreaking. When life comes at us with this type of burden, the only real answer is found in Jesus. Consider another real-life scenario. . . .

The call came in just before midnight. It came from a number I recognized, a good friend of mine in fact. It wasn't the first time I had gotten a similar call, but it was nearing the last. I got dressed and made the short drive to their house and let myself in the unlocked door to find a scene that was becoming a bit too familiar in their home. He was in a back bedroom, slumped on the floor, head in hands openly weeping, the room stinking of stale beer. His wife and kids had locked themselves in a separate room, no doubt hiding out of fear of what this could have escalated into. Nothing physical as of yet, but borderline, while the emotional and mental abuse was simply heart-wrenching. I was there as a mediator, a pressure valve of sorts, just to be sure that everyone was OK. He was sorry, just like he always was when things escalated to a boiling point. His wife was scared, angry, and determined to not let it happen again. The kids were young but knew this shouldn't be considered normal. He didn't want this to be their reality, but all too often we simply can't run from the consequences of the decisions we make. That night was on a path to not end well, but thankfully cooler heads prevailed in the moment. However, in the end that particular marriage didn't survive, leaving so many questions behind.

This chapter is not so much a feel-good portion of this book. However, it is very real, very painful, and pertinent to the lives so many lead. It may seem to be a deviation from where we have been for most of this adventure, but it is imperative that we take a look into this more difficult side of life. These stories are real, albeit slightly altered to protect those involved, and they represent a darker side of life that many dads, moms, husbands, and wives face. Not everything is sunshine and roses, but I am here to tell you that there is hope, and in that hope lies the help that we search for in our most desperate times of need. This chapter contains stories and scenarios that are difficult to read, difficult to understand, and difficult to accept. I have witnessed many of these as a close bystander, and it is necessary to explore some of the difficulties we face in life in order to help point us back to the real answer—our hope and our life in Jesus.

There are cases in this human experience where Dad just isn't around. If you have not yet picked up on it, this book, while directed at dads, holds a special place for moms who function in both roles, for those who have not yet become a dad, and for those looking back and searching for ways to make amends for time lost or mistakes made. I've been there, through difficult times as well. A lost job, financial uncertainty, fear of the unknown, the list goes on. As you've already learned, my wife is a rock, and during my weakest times, she is at her strongest. God enables that in her, and He will do the same in you, no matter if you have your spouse right beside you or if circumstances have dictated otherwise. Our Lord walks with us in the good and the bad, and understandably there are times when we question this. But deep inside the heart of the believer, we know. We know, and we find peace.

Jesus is steadfast. He remains by our side no matter what we may face. In difficult times, times of tragedy, times of loss, or even times of indecision, the one constant we can run to is Jesus. He knows. He cares. He loves you, and He loves me. Too often we try to go about it on our own, no matter what "it" might be; yet He is still patiently waiting to wrap His arms around us in comfort, understanding, and love. If we attempt to deal with tragedy in our lives without Christ, we will find ourselves wandering at best. I know those who have suffered great loss, and in finding the healing they needed in the Lord, they were able to turn tragedy into ministry. Without this direction, it is far too easy for them to fall off the cliff themselves.

Sometimes in this life, things just go sideways. Often it is of our own volition when we either willingly or unwittingly do something stupid. You know, cause and effect, action and reaction, consequences for our decisions and all that. Other times, however, we simply do not understand the hand we have been dealt in life. The question, *Why, God?* is all we can muster. There are those who deem it dangerous to question God. I have a different take on that. When we respectfully and honorably approach our Savior, He welcomes our inquiry. Whether we question or not, He already knows that outcome. He is not offended or surprised when we question Him. He loves us, and He will not forsake us.

"Train up a child in the way he should go and when he is old he will not depart from it." This verse found in Proverbs 22:6 is a promise we can hold on to when our children wander. Our hope, our faith, our only chance lies in the arms of our Lord and Savior, Jesus Christ. Jesus is there with us in that back bedroom. He is there with us at the bedside. He is there with us in the emergency room. He is there with us at the police station. He is there when the money is gone. He is there . . . *period.* Good and bad, thick and thin, easy and hard. There have been times in my life when I felt His presence so intensely that it was palatable, almost tangible. There have been others when He seemed distant, but like the classic poem "Footprints in the Sand," those times when I only saw one set of footprints, it is in those times when He carried me. I didn't even know it, but He was there. If you're that dad, that husband, that mom, that wife, that young person, and you just can't seem to sense His presence right now, rest assured He is there with you. Calmly and tenderly, Jesus is waiting. He is present. He is enough. We can count on one constant in our lives: Jesus.

Chapter 15

LOOKING AHEAD

If you had it to do all over again, what would you change? That is a question we have all been asked at one time or another. For most of us, that is a loaded question. But I prefer to look at it from a different angle. Not, *What would I do differently*, but rather, *What did I learn from it?* Some people say that they wouldn't change a thing from their past, that their mistakes helped to make them who they are today. While there is a modicum of truth to that statement, I take a different stance. Too often people view their past mistakes as excuses. Excuses to not take ownership of the actions that led them down a bad path. Excuses to relapse and fall back into some of their old "mistakes." Excuses to not be a grown-up and move forward in a better way. That may sound harsh, but if you're honest with yourself, you know where I am coming from with that. Our mistakes do not have to define us; they do not have to make us who we are. Rather, if we genuinely look to learn from our mistakes, we can emerge as a better version of ourselves. A better dad, a better husband, a better person.

Do you have any regrets? There's another loaded question, for sure. We all have them, but the key is to not let those regrets define you either. I regret that I quit the tennis team after one year in college. No, I didn't have a career ahead of me in that sport, but at that point in my life, I didn't have the tenacity that developed later, and instead of putting in the work and doing the hard things, I walked away. I have walked away from many, many jobs in my career. One might say I am a quitter based on my career trajectory. I choose to view this differently: I go somewhere, I fix what needs to be fixed, I get bored, and I move on. Much like mistakes, we simply cannot allow our regrets to define who we are today. We must find the strength to learn from them, move on, and strive not to repeat those mistakes that so often lead to regrets as we navigate the path before us.

No crystal ball, no fortune teller, no clairvoyance. What we do have is a promise from God. I touch on this verse multiple times in this book, but it is worthy of each look. Jeremiah 29:11 (my adopted life verse) states, "For I know the plans I have for you, says the Lord. Plans to prosper you and not to harm you. Plans to give you hope and a future." All I can say to that is *wow*! What an amazing promise and hope to hang our hat on day after day.

Recently I have had friends get the news of a difficult health diagnosis. As I talked to them, I was so incredibly encouraged as they live out their faith that God does indeed have a plan for them, even in the dark hours ahead. One of them told me that he takes solace in the fact that the Lord was not taken by surprise by this news. That He knew all those years ago that this trial was coming and in fact that He does know the outcome. There is peace in that, and it applies to each and every one of us, whether things are all fantastic in our lives right now or if we are facing devastating trials. Our God is here, right here beside us, and He knows the plan He has for us. And you know what? It is beautiful.

The same goes for our kids, and we can take comfort in that as well. What lies ahead specifically for us? I certainly don't know, but grandkids would be a top priority on our wish list, for sure! You remember that I told you that I have only held three babies in my life—Lauren, Cam, and Emma. I sure hope the next one is my first grandbaby! I already have plans for him or her, and those plans are indeed full of fun and spoiling them beyond belief. There are also the marriages of our two girls. I'll admit the expense of that scares me a little bit, particularly knowing my girls. But I wait with bated breath for the development of the events that will lead to that, and I continue to pray every single day for Lauren and Emma and the young men that the Lord will one day connect them with. I also pray for those young men as God prepares them for my girls. The blessing of a God-centered marriage cannot have a value stamped on it, but it is one of those things that you certainly know it when you see it, feel it, and live it.

Trudi and I do not have what many would call a bucket list, but we do have things we want to do. Yes, there is travel involved, but there is nowhere to which we are counting the days until we can make it happen. To date, in our empty *nexting* phase, we have had multiple trips to the beach, a trip to Disney, and a trip to Utah where we explored the national parks and were absolutely amazed by the beauty and vastness of God's creation. Beyond grandkids and travel, though, I want to love Trudi more deeply, care for her on a whole new level, and show our grown kids that the many phases of marriage can be and *are* wonderful in their own unique way.

Recently I had an opportunity to apply for a promotion at my current job. Most of my team expected me to apply, thinking I was a great fit for the new role. In fact, some of the corporate decision-makers even asked me about applying for this role. But every time my answer was the same: *no*. No, I am not interested in taking that step in my career at this time. I have been there and done that. I have served as a chief marketing officer, often referred to as the C-Suites, and I have been a vice president over large geographic areas. I have lived that life. Nope, I am not interested in that life at this point. I told anyone who asked that I did not feel like it was God's plan for me *at that time*. I am in a wonderful phase of life, a time where I can spend more time with Trudi, reconnecting and growing even closer to her. Never say never, as we all know, but if and when the time is right, the Lord will lead accordingly.

When I was considering whether or not I should apply, we prayed about it. I already knew the answer, but then I had a bit of a health scare that reminded me what was really important to me at that point in my life. It certainly was not working more, traveling more for work, and taking on the stress and headaches of dealing with corporate expectations on an even higher level. I was happy to walk away, happy to tell those who inquired that, while I remain ambitious and driven, I am just not interested in taking that step right now. Was that a good decision? I guess time will tell, but I have complete peace about it and have happily settled back into a groove of motivating and hopefully inspiring my team to be their very best. Stay tuned on this, as things often change with those who possess leadership titles, which has been the case for me on many occasions. I know beyond any doubt, the Lord truly has a plan for me, and I will patiently do my part to remain in His will and follow said path.

Chapter 16

ADVICE

What is the best advice you have ever been given? Or on the flip side of that, what is the *worst* advice you have ever been given? I would describe both of these as loaded questions. Why, you ask? To me, advice given, particularly when unsolicited, can be misconstrued as something it was never meant to be. Therefore, what was intended as good advice might very well manifest itself in a negative way. That said, you picked up this book and have read it this far, so I will offer you a bit more advice. Remember, the value of said advice is in the hands of the recipient, so carefully consider how you choose to respond.

You buy a book, thinking it might help you improve in some way, but in addition to that, you are reading stories about the life some man has led to this point, focusing on the impact of his wife and kids on him and vice versa. Hopefully you are entertained at a minimum . . . and inspired at best. But I would be remiss if I didn't take a moment in this chapter and simply offer a little advice for the future dads out there. I actually got the idea for this chapter from a gift that Cam and Glori gave me for Christmas. It was a year-long subscription to a storytelling app where each week I am prompted to answer a question submitted by my wife or kids about my life. It provides a nice dovetail as I write this book, and when I was asked the question of what advice would I give future generations of my family, I thought it a perfect addition to this book—a place where my hope and prayers are simply that current and future dads might learn something about being a dad and a place to provide a reflection of the joy I feel in actually being the dad to my kids.

What follows are suggestions for how to build a legacy and live your life forward. Some of these things have been touched on in different parts throughout this book, even if not directly stated, but good advice is worth repeating.

Laugh. This may appear to be an odd place to start, but stay with me on this. We have all heard the old saying that "laughter is the best medicine," and I, for one, think there is wisdom in that statement. One of my absolute favorite things to do in this life is to make my wife laugh. When we were young, we laughed a lot, but as time passed and responsibilities mounted, I found we didn't laugh quite as often. These days, when I can make her genuinely laugh, it simply lights up the room and fills my soul! I don't think we are unique in this pattern, but adding more levity into our lives is definitely a game changer. Laughter is disarming, it is appealing, it is fun, it draws others to you, and in fact, it is healthy. People are indeed drawn to the affable and repelled by curmudgeons. Laughter creates opportunity, and with opportunity comes the ability to make a difference—for yourself and others. Never take that responsibility lightly. No matter what life might throw at you, always find a way, find a time, find a reason . . . to laugh.

Be bold. Stand up for yourself, and put yourself out there. There are certain inherent risks with this advice, principally the chance of failure that accompanies it, but there is no doubt that the reward is worth the risk. As a child, I was terribly introverted and shy. Those who know me now do not believe me, but if you knew me then, you would resoundingly agree. I had no confidence, no boldness, no desire to put myself out there, and, at least in my own mind, no reason to think I ever should do any of those things. Fear was holding me back.

At some point in high school, I changed that approach, and my life vastly improved along with that decision. But know that it was a decision that I had to make; no one could make it for me. God gave me the desire and ability to take that step, and He will do the same for you. Opportunity favors the bold, that is a statistical fact. Put yourself out there, and watch great things happen. If you fail, so what? At least you tried, and at least you learned from it. It is OK—give yourself a break once in a while, and go reap the benefits.

Relax. Do not allow yourself to get or stay stressed out. Relax, and enjoy the journey. It is our default mode while living this human experience to assume the worst. To worry about those things that will never come to fruition. Pour that energy into living your life to its fullest rather than muddling through the "what-ifs." The 1998 Bobby McFerrin hit song "Don't Worry, Be Happy" might oversimplify what I am telling you, but the premise is sound. Trust that our Lord has you in this, and by this, I mean anything that life might throw at you. Take a deep breath, *literally*, and face your fears. There is that word again, *fear*. That drives so many of the negative aspects in our lives, so conquer it and own it, take a breath, and go forward stronger.

Believe. This one sounds simple, but it requires a key component I will circle back around to in a moment. Believe in *God*. Again, He promises us in Hebrews 13:5 that He will never leave us nor forsake us. Jerimiah 29:11 promises us that He does indeed have a plan for us, and it is a good plan—full of hope and a great future. God is good, and He is always right by our side. If at some point this makes it into the hands of someone who has not yet come to know the Lord as their personal Lord and Savior, I ask you to take the time right now to pray for forgiveness and ask Jesus to be the Lord of your life. This does not mean life will always be easy, but it will always be worth it.

Believe in *your family* as well. I understand that not everyone has the joy and privilege of being raised in a loving family environment, but for those who do, no one will ever love you on this earth the way your family loves you. I think of my family as I write this—Trudi, Lauren, Cam, Emma, and now Glori as she has joined us, and my heart swells with love, joy, and pride. I hope that these people believe in me, even half as much as I believe in them. As any of you read this, no matter what you are dealing with, know that I believe in you and that I love you. Faith plays the lead role in belief, no matter where you place your belief. Some say that faith is the opposite of fear. I'm not sure I completely buy that, however. I think fear is also a form of faith; it is just when we place our faith in the wrong place, and it leads to doubt and insecurity. Bold faith is scary in and of itself, but the eternal reward of placing your faith in our Lord is unequivocal, and you will reap untold benefits by practicing your faith with your friends, family, loved ones, and in every aspect of your life today. You just never know whose life will be changed by the faith you live.

Passion. Energy, drive, and passion. These three things are what I look for in the people I surround myself with. By *energy*, I simply mean one's ability to lift the room when they enter. Not bouncing off the walls and getting on people's nerves—just the opposite. People feel this kind of positive energy that all of us can exude, but all too often we adopt a brooding, negative energy that inevitably drives people away. *Drive* is not confined to our career path; rather, I mean apply it to every single aspect of our lives. Be driven to find the good in others. Be driven to work harder and smarter. Be driven to do good in this life. Be driven to make a difference. Again, this is a personal decision that we must all make. It isn't always easy to adopt a driven mentality, but the difference you can make is immeasurable. That leads me to *passion*. I've always had the prayer that our kids would find their passion and pursue it. I never once cared if it was sports, academics, fine arts, or simply the pursuit of a better life for themselves and those around them. Just be passionate about something, and never lose it. Passion leads to energy, which enhances one's drive, so you might see the method to my madness in how I delivered this. There have been times in my life when my passion has exuded so strongly from me that I simply couldn't contain it. While at other times, one would have to search desperately to even see if I was passionate about anything at all. My passion and love for my family is what drives me today, and I never want anyone to be able to question that.

Love. You were probably wondering when I would get to this one, right? The greatest gift we can give others is to love them. To unselfishly love without expecting anything in return is difficult,

ADVICE

to say the least, but what is life without love? We all want to be loved, and I am blessed beyond measure with the way that my wife and kids love me. My wife is the purest example I know of putting others ahead of herself and is a standard I strive to achieve each day in my life. I hope that our kids will learn to emulate her love and unselfishness, even as I pursue her same level in these areas. But she just gets it, and my family is truly blessed as a result. Take this advice now: *love unselfishly*, and not only will those around you be blessed, but you will find yourself to be truly blessed as well. This is not about what you may or may not receive in return; it is quite the opposite. It is about giving of yourself so that others know they are loved. Christ perfectly exemplified this, and while we will never truly be able to achieve His level of love, the bar is set, so go forward with that in mind.

There are a few thoughts for my family and for you to ponder as we go forward. Always remember that failure doesn't define you, friends do not define you, and financial success does not define you. Who you are and how you treat others, living out your faith, that is a definition I hope others will adopt for who they are. I hope that my legacy will be one of success but not necessarily in worldly terms; rather, it is my prayer that my family first, and others within my circle of influence as well, will look back on my life and say without a doubt, *He loved me. He wasn't perfect by any means, but he loved me, and he genuinely cared about me.* Leave a legacy of love, and there you have my definition of success. Each of these areas of life that I have discussed builds upon one another, culminating with love. Put yourself aside, and love those around you. Again, you just never know the difference you might make.

Chapter 17

ON SECOND THOUGHT...

Originally I thought this would be the last chapter in this book, but if you stick with me just a moment longer, you will see why I built that out a bit differently.

So often our first thought is a knee-jerk reaction—sometimes angry, at times emotional, quite often wrong, and yet sometimes beautiful. Take, for instance, how you respond to being stuck in traffic.

It is a Tuesday afternoon, and you leave work around your normal time. You have a bit of a commute home, but that commute is the same each day. Today, however, is just not your day. Immediately you merge into traffic, and your patience is already shot. Everyone on the road is an idiot, maybe even including you! Nothing is really any different today than normal, but all of these idiots are really grating on your nerves, and you remain convinced that you are the only human on the planet that has any clue how to operate a motorized vehicle. Eventually you navigate the treacherous path home, and upon arrival, you know your mindset isn't where it should be, but you really don't care. Your wife doesn't greet you at the door, your kids don't come running, screaming, "Daddy's home! Daddy's home!" and even your dog simply ignores you. *Choose your next words and actions very carefully*, as the rest of your night and maybe the next couple of days may depend on it! Unfortunately, you take the low road and complain about everything and everyone, including your innocent wife, kids, and dog. I warned you, with that response your night might not go as planned, so here you sit all alone with nothing left to do but read this book you picked up a few weeks back. Could be a long night.

As is most often the case, you make it through the night, and you make it through the next workday as well, so you enter the afternoon commute once again. Today, for whatever reason, those idiots don't seem to be quite as irritating. The flow seems much faster, and they are even playing songs on the radio that you can sing along with. Your commute seems to fly by, and when you pull into your driveway your dog is already waiting by your car to welcome you home, tail wagging so hard it seems his whole body wags with him. Your beautiful bride opens the door to greet you with a big hug and a kiss and wants to hear all about your day. Your kids greet you as if you've been gone for a month and beg you to come out and play in the backyard. Life is good. You are the king of the hill, the hero of your own story. This is how it is supposed to be, right?

Well, I hate to break it to you, but every bit of this in each scenario is on *you*, not on the traffic patterns or how you are greeted when you get home. It is about your mindset, and you are the only one who can control that. The traffic was the same on both days. Face it, it sucks most every day, but it was how you viewed it and reacted to it that was different. It changed your whole approach to your commute and how you viewed your reception when you arrived home. It even affected how you reacted to those drivers surrounding you, making it personal when indeed it really had nothing to do with you. We all know our kids usually do want to play when dad gets home, but you didn't view it that way due to your bad-traffic mindset day. Your wife will always greet you, maybe not in the iconic, 1950s-era method you envisioned, but even that is impacted by your mindset put in place by your traffic issues. And come on, we all know your dog is always glad to see you, no matter what the circumstance. It all revolves around your perception of these things, and that is based on your mindset.

My advice here? Allow some time for self-reflection. How about a little dose of self-awareness, which is something that is in short supply these days. Apply a little of that emotional intelligence you claim to have along with a heavy dose of the aforementioned self-awareness before you point the finger at traffic, or even worse, at your wife, kids, and dog. Whether you realize it or not, they are counting on you to be their constant, their even-keeled household staple, and yes, in some cases, their knight in shining armor. Picture that guy: all clad head to toe in galvanized steel; a few scratches and scrapes blemishing the polished metal from times past when you had to save the day; a plume of feathers mounted atop your majestic helmet with the facemask drawn; one foot propped up on an expertly placed stone; staring off into the middle distance with those deep, searching eyes and firmly set jaw; contemplating all the ways you can save the world, all while the sun gently sets in the background. Nice shot, right? Maybe your family doesn't see you that way on a regular basis, but there are times when they do. We as dads and husbands should ascribe to be that guy, no matter how unrealistic it may seem. We must set the stretch goal and, again, not just be the hero of our own stories but indeed be the hero to theirs. Use that eventful and timely commute—whether it is ten minutes or two hours—to reset your focus, put the frustrations of the day behind you, and think ahead on how you plan to honor your wife and kids, and yes, even your faithful friend, your pup, when you get home. Take the time to put aside your workday, no matter how it went, and simply love your family. Believe me, this is experience talking, and I pray that you hear me and don't make the same mistakes I have made over the years by bringing all of that baggage home with you and subsequently taking it out on those who love you most. This leads me back to the title of this chapter: *On second thought.* . . .

That second thought can be the one that matters most. How many times in your life have you said to yourself, *On second thought* . . . , and you went on to make a better decision, to do that thing you thought you couldn't do, to accomplish that one thing that you found elusive on first thinking of it? While these are wonderful second thought scenarios, there is more. And this *more* is so much better.

With your second thought comes great power. With your second thought comes great clarity. With your second thought comes great appreciation. With your second thought comes great wisdom. So often in our lives, our second thought leads us back to Jesus, and in Jesus truly comes all things great. I certainly can't speak for you, but I'm pretty sure I'm right on this: too many of us on too many occasions relegate Jesus to our second thought. Can you imagine the joy, peace, and wonder if we adjust our thought process by just that tiny bit of nuance, and lean into Jesus with our first thought, with our *every* thought? The thought of Jesus simply isn't enough. We all know plenty of people who have Jesus thoughts but fail to see Jesus results time after time. The biggest difference here is those few inches between your heart and your head—truly tucking Jesus into your heart and life versus just having the head knowledge of His greatness and His peace that passes all understanding.

As I reflect on my life throughout this book and beyond, I am ashamed to admit that as a believer, far too often I have relegated Jesus to second-thought status. He allows me to do this, and thankfully He welcomes me back into His fold with open arms, even when I have failed Him miserably. I would be remiss if I didn't take this opportunity to share the Good News of Jesus and salvation through Him. Face it, we have all failed, and none of us are worthy of the grace, mercy, and forgiveness that is offered through Christ, but those very things are simply there waiting for us to claim if we turn from our sins and ask forgiveness, knowing that we have the promise of eternal life in the arms of Jesus. That very thing is what inspires me to strive to live a life worth telling stories about for my wife, my kids, myself, and those within my circle of influence.

All those who choose Christ will join me, praising Him for eternity, and that is where true hope is found. I trust you have this assurance in your life, but if not, I assure you it is not too late. God's Word is still the all-time bestseller and available at your fingertips right now. Read it, study it, talk about it, ask questions about it, live it, and ultimately ask for the forgiveness that we do not deserve but is so willingly given. We may not know each other on this earth, but as believers we will have the opportunity to spend eternity together, and that is the path to true peace and joy. Talk about a legacy for my family! That is my prayer and where my true joy lies to this day and as we press forward.

Chapter 18

LEGACY

We arrive at the final chapter of this book, the namesake behind the title and the driving force behind why I choose to pour out my heart to you on these pages. We've come full circle on the whole *developing dad* concept, and if you're still with me, I hope to finish strong for you and inspire you to go and be a better version of yourself. After all, no matter where you are in *your* phase of life, you are still developing just like me.

For many years, I have heard this saying: "How you do anything is how you do everything." I do not know who to attribute that to, but I think it holds a truth that we can all build upon. Think about how a sports team practices. Yes, practice does indeed influence how you play, so don't you owe it to your teammates to give it your all, knowing full well that how you do anything is how you do everything? How you purposefully develop yourself as a dad and as a husband will have an infinite influence on your family tree and the legacy that follows. That is a heavy statement, so take it seriously, and know that you're not done yet.

Legacy is a big word and one that I take very seriously. By definition, it means the long-lasting impact of a person's life. So many mornings I wake up, look in the mirror, and think to myself, *That can't be right!* Indeed, time marches on and, with that, hopefully the amount of wisdom and influence I garner increases with my ever-increasing wrinkles and gray hair. As a dad, I am convinced that there is no more important role that we can play than just that—being a dad. There are good dads out there, there are deadbeat dads out there. There are those who really do mean well, yet they fall so far short that their intent is lost on those around them. There are those who appear to have it all together, but a quick peek behind the curtain would reveal a fraud that rivals the wizard behind the curtain in *The Wizard of Oz*. But most of us are on a pretty even playing field. We want to do right by our family. We want to provide for and protect them. We love them wholeheartedly, even if we are sometimes distracted and it doesn't shine through.

Writing this book has shone a bright spotlight on me, at least in my eyes, focusing on how much better I *could have been*. I have regrets that I will never live down, but today is a new day and one where I can choose to take a different path. Robert Frost wrote, "Two roads diverged in the woods, and I—I chose the one less traveled by, and that has made all the difference."[2] Let's unpack that a bit further and how it relates to the legacy we leave.

The general consensus on the meaning of this quote follows the thought line of being a nonconformist. *My life is a bit different from others because of the choices I make*, or, *I don't follow the crowd; rather, I do things my own way.* I think these interpretations are spot on, and maybe that is why I like that quote. I have always chosen to be a little different, to do things my way, to be unique in my own right—all of this for the good or for the bad (maybe that is still yet to be determined). I find it hard to adopt almost any template. Whether at work or in my personal life, when someone tells me that something must be done in a particular manner, following a step-by-step process that always guarantees success, to say I am a bit doubtful would be an understatement. Each of us is unique, created in the image of God but wonderfully different and unique in our very own ways. Taking a different path can lead you on new adventures you never would have imagined, especially if you just keep your head down and follow

---

2. Robert Frost, "The Road Not Taken" (1916). Public domain.

the guy in front of you. That is one of the points of this book—to encourage you to be more of *you*. Accentuate the positives in your life while downplaying the negatives. None of us are perfect, but that doesn't mean we should give up trying to achieve that. Earlier I mentioned that phrase—I try and I try and I try, and I will always continue to try. Sometimes that is the best we can give, and in the end, if we give our best, there will be much happiness to follow. Going your own way doesn't always lead to success, happiness, or even one accord in your own household, but as we have all heard for most of our lives, if you do the right thing, you just can't go wrong. At least try, and go all in.

That said, during one of our trips to Disney, I chose to pick a fight with a stranger . . . sort of. No, there were no hands thrown, and I'll let you be the judge if I did the right thing or not. The point is, I made a choice, and once that was done, I was all in.

In the evenings at the Magic Kingdom, there is a spectacular light and fireworks show at the castle. People line up in that area long before the start time, and we choose to do the same, picking a spot beside a young mom and her two kids on the edge of the designated walkway so no one could block their view. We settled in over an hour before showtime as had the family next to us. With about ten minutes to go, a man and his new bride walked up and squeezed into the marked off spot directly in front of this young family, blocking the little kids' view. I looked at the mom, and she just shook her head and slumped her shoulders. One thing I simply cannot tolerate is injustice. Just do not take advantage of other people. I think this is a trait I learned from my own dad, but I can't stand to see people treated wrongly, with disrespect, or taken advantage of. So I decided to step in. I walked over to the guy and told him he had to move. He responded by saying, "Make me." My wife immediately knew this was not going to go well. Our kids were all with us and at this point all young adults. But they were definitely interested in where this was going.

I told the guy that he could not stand there, blocking the view of this family who had been here over an hour. He proceeded to ask me if there was a law against it. What a punk. I stepped a bit closer as there were literally thousands of people all around. I told him there might not be a law against it other than the law of human decency. He said again, "Make me move." I responded by telling him to do the right thing and move on. I also told him I didn't even know these people, so he asked why I even cared then. "It is simply the right thing to do," I responded, and I told him that he knew he was wrong by breaching the protocol of just doing the right thing. He said, "Why don't you call the Disney police on me then? Otherwise I'm staying right here." At this point my wife and her wisdom won out as she told me to step away, which was followed by this lady I didn't even know telling me it was OK. Notice I said that Trudi *told* me, not *asked* me. She knows me all too well and knew this was not a healthy situation under development.

I looked at this guy, then at his wife, and I told her she was in for a long life with a jerk like this, and she should rethink her life decisions. OK, I didn't *actually* say that, but I did look at him and tell him that he knew he was wrong, that he was being a real jerk, and that if he had any thread of common decency in his life he would move on. He said he was going to stay, and there was nothing I could do about it.

In reality I could have moved him out, I could have had the Disney police move him out, but having said my peace and done what I thought was right, I chose to step away. That young mom leaned over to me and thanked me for what I did, even though it ultimately did no good. We resituated ourselves so her kids had a good view, and guess what? A family of near giants came in as the show started and positioned themselves directly in front of the guy and his wife. I couldn't help but laugh out loud at this turn of events as I watched them both try to stand on their tip-toes and find a viewing lane. I am confident that my response to this was not particularly mature and certainly not Christ-like, but I just couldn't help myself as the old saying of what goes around comes around showed up and showed out in this situation.

Did I make the right decision to insert myself into a situation that didn't involve me? Did I do enough to even make a difference? Who knows, but to me it was simply the right thing to do, and I could not help myself. It is my hope that my wife and kids experienced a little bit of pride with my actions, knowing my intent was to simply do the right thing. That little mom and her family . . . I'll never see them again, but just maybe some hope in humanity was restored for her simply by choosing a path less traveled that night.

So how does this sticky situation apply to this book, to you, and to your own legacy? We make our own choices, so I challenge you to do the following:

- **Choose to be a good human.** It is always a choice to be a good person and ultimately to be a good dad. Make that choice.
- **Choose to go the extra mile.** You just don't know what someone is going through until you have walked that extra mile in their shoes.
- **Choose the high road** (maybe the one *less traveled*). Oh, what adventures await!
- **Choose to win.** Winning has many contexts, but doing so with grace, dignity, and the highest of ethical standards is a reward in and of itself.
- **Choose to do the right thing.** No additional commentary is needed here.
- **Choose to genuinely care** for and love those within your circle of influence. Yes, that starts with your family, the place where your legacy will be truly revealed and remembered for generations to come.

Your legacy is built on purpose, not on chance. Some years back, I chose to write a personal mission statement. I gave you this as I opened our time together in this book, but it is worth unpacking just a bit before we go. This statement outlines a significant part of my life, and it seems fitting to reiterate that with you in this segment. It goes as follows:

> *To help others lead their best life possible, if they only knew it existed.*

This is a two-part mission statement, and it must be pursued purposefully. First, *help others lead their best life possible.* In reality, although it comes first in my statement, this is actually the long road that one chooses to follow. The second part—*if they only knew it existed*—now that is the tricky part! From one relationship to another, helping others identify that part is a difficult undertaking. Once someone truly understands that there is a best life out there, then they can be intentional in their pursuit, and anything I can help them do along that path is rewarding and fulfilling to me as a part of who I am.

I first learned of this concept of legacy, to the point where it really had an impact in my life, from Trudi's dad, Mr. Charlie. The way he lived and loved and the way he was loved by his family. All of this was truly inspiring to me and caused me to begin the thought process that led not only to changes in my own life but to this book actually coming to fruition. Every name that has been mentioned, as well as so many others implied, has played a part in the development of the dad I am, the husband I am, and the life I lead. I pose this question to you: *Who is developing you?* This development is an ongoing process, one where we will never truly arrive. My teams that I work with often hear me say, "The finish line is our starting point." If the meaning of that isn't clear, allow me to shine the spotlight on it for you. If you view the finish line as your actual end-point, who knows what you might miss if you stop there? Who knows what wonder awaits you when you go that proverbial extra mile, when you give that extra bit of effort, when you push beyond normal expectations? That is where the magic happens, so never sell yourself short.

If you've been paying attention, you've seen me mention this phrase a few times throughout these pages: always strive to live a life worth telling stories about. Storytelling is an art unto itself and something I thoroughly enjoy doing. But if I don't have anything worth telling you about, then where have I gone wrong? Living a life worth telling stories about is a challenge as much as it is an opportunity. Take a chance, spend the money, attempt something new, love someone deeper—whatever it takes to create a great story. Then don't be afraid to tell it.

I consider myself a bit of a storyteller. I've had many people tell me over the years that I am quite accomplished at it. That probably only means I run my mouth too much, but I choose to take it as a compliment. Storytelling might not be Trudi's greatest attribute, and when I tell her to "land the plane" it usually doesn't go very well for me! But the way she lives her life is the stuff of legends, so I'll gladly step in and help tell her story for her, usually whether she wants me to or not.

Along with storytelling comes the ubiquitous inclusion of great quotes. There are as many great quotes out there as the circumstances that warrant utilizing them, but one that always comes to mind for me is this one first attributed to Henry Ford, revealed shortly after his death in 1947: "Whether you think you can, or you think you can't . . . you're right!"[3] Think about that for just a minute. It goes hand in hand with what I already introduced you to—how you do anything is how you do everything. I'll remind you again that mindset matters, no matter the circumstance. As dads, we are called to make hard choices and do hard things. That is not just a recommendation; no, it is mandatory. And nobody ever said it would be easy, but yes, it will be worth it. I implore you to not take this responsibility lightly, but also do not see it as a burden. Rather, take the heavy yoke upon your shoulders, and run the race set before you with perseverance, strength, love, and determination.

I pray that God will give me more of what matters in this life and less of what doesn't. More time with my family, more memories made with Trudi and our kids, and more differences made in the lives of others. Andy Stanley once said, "Your greatest contribution to the kingdom of God may not be something you do but rather someone you raise."[4] I know that is the case for me, having raised three fantastic kids alongside the best wife a man could ever ask for. Raising your children will quite possibly be the most difficult thing you will ever do, the most difficult thing you will ever accomplish. But oh, what an accomplishment that is.

No matter where you fall on the spectrum of your journey of being a dad—your kids are grown and out of the house, you have little ones running all around you every day, or even if you have not yet been blessed with your first child—take heart. The journey before you still carries with it some of the most amazing times you could ever imagine in your life. As you evaluate where you are along this

---
3. Quote likely from Henry Ford, although not verified through the Henry Ford Museum archives' exhaustive list of Ford quotes.
4. Andy Stanley via Twitter, April 17, 2013. Used with permission.

path, I encourage you to live each day to its fullest, never letting a moment pass you by. As you grow as a dad, you will come to realize a sobering fact—one that is worth tucking away in your memory and pulling out at each stop along the journey: **you will never fully arrive**. Your love for your family will never wain, never diminish, never cease to amaze even you. As you live your life, choose to soak in each moment, stop and smell the proverbial roses, and slow down long enough to realize this is indeed a journey. It is more about enjoying the ride than arriving at your destination.

You may wonder why I would choose to give you this peek behind the curtain into my life and the life of my family. Well, this isn't about trying to show how good, how bad, or how ugly my attempts at being a loving dad and husband are. No, rather it is an honest look at the life of someone who simply tries to be a little bit better each day. A little bit better in my walk with the Lord, a little bit better in how I love my wife and kids, a little bit better in leading those within my circle of influence . . . just a little bit better, period. This book is for my family. My wife, my kids, my extended family—there is no doubt about that. But there is a part of me that hopes that maybe just one young dad will come across this title and decide to pick it up. Hopefully, somewhere within the timeframe when he is reading, there will be one small thing that he can pick up on and think, *You know what? That sounds like a great idea!* And from there, he will do something, change something, or love someone a little bit better. If that is the case, I have accomplished my goal in writing this book. It isn't just about raising great kids, it is about raising kids to become great adults. It isn't just about the life lessons we can teach but also about how we can continue to grow, continue to improve, and continue to build that legacy we want to leave as a dad. Living a life of legacy is a heavy lift but one I am totally up for and in for. For the developing dad part, I know I am still, and I always will be a work in progress. I own that, and I love that. Remember, we never fully arrive, but the difference we can make along the way is simply immeasurable.

I mentioned the importance of quotes in a good story earlier in this chapter. Allow me to give you a couple more that continue to impact my life and help me retain my focus on the here and now. So many authors have used this one in a variety of contexts, so I will do the same. As great as things may be today, never forget that if indeed you allow it to be, *the best is yet to come.* If you truly believe this, take heart no matter what your current situation looks like. You may be on the mountaintop, or you may be in the valley, but life rolls just like that, and knowing that there is hope in what lies ahead is an encouragement I want you to take seriously.

As I write notes of encouragement to the teams I work with, I adopt a sign-off that most of them take very little notice of in the context where I use it. But I've had some tell me that this closing is actually *their* favorite leadership quote. I find that humbling and encouraging, but it is more than just a sign-off. It is my promise to them, and it is my implied promise to Trudi and our kids as well. If taken seriously, it is quite a commitment, and I do indeed take it seriously. As I close our time together, I offer you this same statement, this same commitment, this same promise. For my family, it is more than implied, it is my faithful promise to them and something I am committed to more than ever in my life. It is simple yet binding, and it comes from my heart. With that, here it comes, and I offer it to you for adoption into your world as a dad as well. Never forget . . . **I'm right here with you.** Through thick and thin, the good times and the bad, the ups and downs, and yes, the times of tragedy and exuberance, that fact remains. I am right here with you.

And just in case there is any doubt remaining . . . *I sure do love my family!*

ABOUT THE AUTHOR

Trent Presley is a full-time husband, full-time father, full-time believer, and yes, at a minimum, a part-time idiot. He constantly and consistently strives to be a better version of himself, day in and day out. In his quest to help people lead their best lives possible, he attempts to lead through inspiration and encouragement. The mistakes he has made will too often be replicated in the future but not for lack of trying to find a better path. As a voracious reader and one always on a journey to be a better leader, he finds himself constantly seeking ways to improve himself so that in turn, he can make a difference in the lives of others.

Trent is someone who genuinely wants to do the right thing, but all too often falls short. His family, the inspiration for this entire book, continues to be gracious and loving, even humoring him in his often lame attempts at situational humor. His hope is that by taking the time to read the antics, mistakes, stories, successes, and failures outlined in this book, you will find yourself inspired to keep on trying. He has stated that this book is for his family, even for himself as the culmination of a life-long dream to tell this story. If indeed a young father picks this up along the way and finds himself thinking, *You know, if this guy can do this, I can too!* then consider it mission accomplished.

Trent has been writing for years but not in the format of this book. The teams he has coached in his business life have been subjected to his writings through all-too-lengthy emails on a weekly basis. He's always been told he should turn those submissions into a book. Hmm, we'll see about that. Stay tuned for renditions to follow where he hopes to publish more in a variety of formats and manuscripts.

He signs off at work with a phrase he picked up from author Ron Kitchens, which summarizes how he attempts to live each day: *Always forward.* That sign-off carries with it the promise of something more, something new, something better, and is in and of itself a mindset reminder of the greatness that awaits. His favorite phrase

ABOUT THE AUTHOR

is simple and sums up his philosophy in life. It was alluded to in chapter seventeen but is worthy of one more look as we come to a close. In all cases, in all circumstances, in all situations, no matter the good or the bad, stay tuned, stay engaged, stay focused, and never forget: *the best is yet to come!*

BOOK RECOMMENDATIONS

As a voracious reader, I recommend this same habit to you. I have an amazing library of books from so many of my favorite authors, and often people ask me for recommendations. Here are those currently in my top ten, realizing I continue to read, and this list can evolve and grow over time. If you're counting, this list is a top ten plus a bonus, so there are eleven, but I didn't want to eliminate any of these as my recommendation to the start of your reading journey. You will find that each of these authors have multiple publications available, so as you read one, go digging into that author, and go find another. It is a proven fact that leaders read. Leaders continually learn. And no matter if you are looking to lead better at home, at work, or at life in general, I am confident you should pick up these books and start your journey. Enjoy!

The Noticer, Andy Andrews

She Calls Me Daddy, Robert Woglemuth

Uniquely You, Ron Kitchens

The Power of Change, Craig Groeschel

The Six Types of Working Genius, Pat Lencioni

The Energy Bus, Jon Gordon

Essentialism, Greg McKeown

Love Does, Bob Goff

Chase the Lion, Mark Batterson

Start With Why, Simon Sinek

The Tipping Point, Malcolm Gladwell

Printed in the USA
CPSIA information can be obtained
at www.ICGtesting.com
LVHW021912260924
792274LV00016B/39/J